Have a Great Idea, But No Money?
Do not Let that Stop You!

DOING BUSINESS WITHOUT MONEY

Dr. Suresh Haware

PRABHAT PAPERBACKS

Published by
PRABHAT PAPERBACKS
4/19 Asaf Ali Road,
New Delhi-110 002 (INDIA)
e-mail: prabhatbooks@gmail.com

ISBN 978-93-5266-141-1
DOING BUSINESS WITHOUT YOUR MONEY
by Dr. Suresh Haware

Edition
First, 2017

Price
₹ 200.00 (Rupees Two Hundred only)

Printed at
Yash Printographics, Noida

Dedicated to
The inspiring memory of Bharat Ratna
Hon Dr. A.P.J. Abdul Kalam,
a renowned Scientist, whose proclamation
"Dreams are not those that are seen
in the deep sleep,
But the Dreams are those Aims,
which does not allow you to sleep"
made every Indian to Dream Big.

Foreword

I have known Dr. Suresh Haware for the past 20 years. His journey is immense and still going very strong. From a Chemical engineer to a Nuclear scientist– working with one of the most brilliant mind of modern India– Late Dr. A.P.J. Abdul Kalam's team, then moving into Business; and tomorrow only sky is the limit. In all his activities, his focus has always been the Good of Mankind.

What he shares in this book is his experiences. He being a first generation businessman in his family, his experience of all that he faced while initiating his business, running the business, maintaining the business and lastly expanding the business.

As rightly said it is the attitude of person that matters– whether he wants to do job or wants to start his own business.

What Dr. Haware conveys is– It is the 'Idea' the 'Seed' that matters. If the Seed is right, people will come forward to water it, see it grow and reap the fruits. So, if you have a business mind, a great idea, persistence and integrity then there is no reason why you shall not succeed in you endeavours.

This book will help in clearing your confusions and

set you on the path of success. Support will be available to those who deserve it.

I am Happy that Dr. Suresh Haware has, after the success of his book in Marathi, not only translated it in English but has also improved on the previous edition. Because all should have access to a great book.

My best wishes to Dr. Haware and happy reading to all.

— Dr. Manohar Joshi
M.A., L.L.B., Ph D.

Member of Parliament - Rajya Sabha 2006-2012
Speaker - Lok Sabha 2002-2004
Minister - Government of India 1999-2002
Chief Minister - Maharashtra 1995-1999
Leader of Opposition - Maharashtra 1990-1991
Mayor - Mumbai 1976-1977

Preface

'Now It Can Be Told.'

I learnt a great deal from what I experienced in the last twenty-five years, overcoming all the obstacles that came my way after I became a businessman. I wanted to share all these experiences. Hence this book! Sharing (the experiences) with several people, I realized that the first-generation businessmen had a lot to learn from these. There is a famous saying that "Those who learn from their own experience are common people, but those who learn from others' experience are known to be clever." I am sure, many people will become wiser after reading this book.

I feel intensely that the new businessmen and the numerous youth, intending to become businessmen, will find these words of experience very useful. I have met many such youth, spoken to them, understood from them their fears-doubts and accordingly penned this book. Hence, I feel that this book will be of great utility to all of them.

This book will also facilitate a positive view towards business and businessmen by the rulers, government officials, society and all others, as it has been specifically stated in this book that businessmen are the "creator of wealth of the nation", meaning, they are the producers of the nation's wealth.

Most important of all, after running a business for so many years, coming in contact with thousands of businessmen, getting to know their experiences and feelings, I took up writing this book after a voice from deep within (me) urged that 'now all these experiences must be told.' I wish, trust and expect that this book will be very well accepted and (my) objective would be served in the very first chapter I have tried to explain – what is the meaning of others' money and the meaning of doing business without money. Later it has been duly elucidated in the other chapters too. I have presented this book to inculcate this new perspective among the general public that 'Business has to be run on others' money.' I appeal to you to understand this clearly. If you are able to bring to use even a fraction of this, you will yourself realize the extent of truth in what I say. I am not narrating any philosophy that is out of this world: I am presenting this philosophy of mine as a summary of what I have experienced and learnt from others.

Prior to this, I have placed this subject at many business seminars. They were appreciated every time. Having heard this, a friend experimented whether this philosophy was useful and eventually he became a businessman. Presently, his project is taking a good shape. He had no money when he started, but today his earnings are substantial and even his investor is reaping good returns. Both are delighted. When I once placed this philosophy at a business meet, a senior businessman came forward to second what I proposed. I am not a traditional businessman. Nor do I have a heritage of business backing me.

I am a first-generation businessman and I learnt as first-generation businessmen learn to surmount obstacles and pitfalls. No books are available to make one an expert in business. It is also not true that one can do business by learning from books. Just as one has to plunge into the water to swim and cannot swim by reading its theory in books, so also in the case of doing business. Without practically doing a business, one can neither learn nor do it. Hence, I have presented this book in a very practical format.

We have often read that gathering the best people and taking care of them is business, meaning thereby that the 'People is Business'. But in my opinion, the definition of business is much broader. Hence, I find 'Relation is Business' more apt. Now, people do not mean that an enterprise or business can be run by merely gathering people. A relation has to be created with them. Meaning that once he buys goods from you or invested in your business and has a good experience, he will come back again. By thus coming back repeatedly, you create a relation with him. Then he is ready to do whatever you say. You will thus experience the principle of 'Relation is Business'. Once a relationship is created with many people, a series is formed. This is called 'Network'. Then we will have to further state that 'Network is Business'.

These are the steps for the growth of a business. There are several misconceptions among people about business, such as – one has to cheat a lot or do fraudulent acts to do business. But through experience one realizes that business can be done honestly. Falsehood does not last long. But I will state emphatically that one should have full faith on this principle. We enter into several legal deals in the course of doing business. We do Memorandum of Understandings (MoUs), agreements and so on. But in business the honesty of the people entering into the agreement is most valued. Through this only the worth of one's word enhances. The weight of one's word increases and then business commences on the strength of such a word. You will be surprised that it is a fact that big deals are struck merely on the trust of a word.

Tata's Nano factory in Bengal ran into trouble and it had to be shifted elsewhere and a big question of 'what to do' confronted Ratan Tata then. One day he received a SMS from the then Chief Minister of Gujarat, Narendra Modi, stating 'you are welcome to Gujarat'. On that single SMS, Tata shifted his Nano car factory from Singur (Bengal) to Gujarat and started the production of cars there. Such is the value of 'a word'. When several people get the experience of truthfulness and fairness (about a product/company/service), a business brand is created. Goods are then sold only on the strength of the brand. But years and years of honest dealings go into this brand building.

Many have the misconception that a brand is built through aggressive advertising and the consistent hammering of advertisements. But this is not true. Advertising only introduces the product. But trust is built through dealing and having good experience. Hence, brand is not one name of advertising, but the trust behind that name. Also note that Tata does not need to advertise as much as some companies have to. Tata products sell by their name – be it the ordinary tea that one starts drinking on waking up in the morning, soap, toothpaste, salt in the meals, the car that is used the whole day or the bulb that is switched off before going to sleep at night. It is mentioned herein that Brand Building is very important.

Obstacles and impediments will come in business. They should be greeted and not feared. For, they put our true capabilities to test. Therefore, they should be taken as 'Blessings in Disguise'. Impediments can be of various kinds, e.g. economic, legal, about manufacturing, about taxes, about staff and administrative. There is a solution to all problems (impediments), we have to find them. Just as, illness has to be first diagnosed, so also the problems. Diagnosing impediments means finding the reasons (causes). Once the cause is known, the solution too is certainly found. Many a time it so happens that for problems of legal issues, economic solutions are sought or for economic problems, legal solutions are sought and thereby causing more complications.

Treatment should be done on the advice of the right expert. Meaning that it is so much a matter of ifs and buts that we will be forced to agree that it would be apt to address a legal-related issue with a legal remedy or solve a domestic strife with a dose of affection (sense of belongingness). Yet, there cannot be a comprehensive answer to all impediments. However, issues, impediments should not be ignored. A small hole too can sink a large ship. Controversy in business is not new. But as far as possible, it will be wise to seek a pragmatic solution. Here, our ego should not come in the way. Swearing 'to teach a lesson' has no place in business. Remember that sometimes it is imperative to take one step backward to surge forward.

An effort has been made here to differentiate between Cost and Value. A long sustaining journey has to be based on values. Values are very significant in establishing a business. Let us understand this difference with a striking example. In order to make his educated unemployed son do some work, the father decided to give him ₹ 2/- everyday. It is decided that he should go out, roam the market, try to get a job and doing these spend ₹ 1/-and drop the balance ₹ 1/- in the well of the house after returning home. The son takes ₹ 2/- daily and while coming home drops ₹ 1/- in the well. One day he gets a job. He does a lot of work. With his effort he earns ₹ 2/-. Hearing this, the father is very pleased. He casually asks him to drop ₹ 1/- out of his earning in the well. The son clearly refuses to do that, stating, "I have earned these ₹ 2/- by toiling hard and shedding my sweat. I will not drop this in the well." The ₹ 2/- given by the father had a value of only ₹ 2/-. But the ₹ 2/- earned by the son with hard work though has the same cost but is invaluable. This is the difference between Cost and Value. Therefore, Business must be Value based.

Today, all businessmen have one experience, i.e. of administrative scrutiny. There is nothing like One Time Tax in our country. For people doing business there are many types of taxes. These taxes torment the businessmen. The TDS meaning Tax Deducted at Source, these people conduct raids (at business places). Then come the Income Tax survey. After that is done, the same department's Search and Seizure raid is done, then Service Tax, Sales Tax, VAT and so many people come and torment by looking at them and behaving with them as if they are thieves. Look, how funny it is! The government of the country is run on taxes. We are, in fact, the taxpayers, who run the government, meaning we are the owners. All the officials and employees of the government are public servants. Yet they raid us. That means the servants raid the owners and allege that taxes have been robbed. What do we call this? This should change. The spirit of business should pervade all over the nation. Businessmen should be revered. I am not raising this as an individual matter, but this will create an atmosphere of love for business and appreciation of businessmen among the public.

Hence, all tax raids should be stopped completely. There may be mischievous elements, true. But then you have e-connectivity and just sitting in office, everything can be viewed. What I mean to say is that the technological solution should be looked for.

Whatever we earn is given to us by society. Whatever is with us, ultimately belong to the society and hence should go back to society. So long as Capital – be it small or big – is with us, we are its trustees; we should keep this in mind always. Thus, the concept of Corporate Social Responsibility came into being. Through this, considering the needs of the society, some portion of the profits earned should be utilized to meet these needs. These should be done, not as a (charity) giver, but as a doer. 'I should do them as a duty'. In this spirit, the society will look upon businessmen with more sensitivity.

Finally, we have to bear in mind, as an Indian saying goes as '*Sar Salamat to Pagadi Pachas*' meaning thereby, 'if the head is secure, it could sport 50 turbans'. That means whatever we have to achieve, is possible, with this physical body. Hence, we should always be very aware of our health. Just as, if the downtime of a project is increased then the loss too increases, profit reduces, and so is the case with our health. Hence, taking care of their health, businessmen should be prepared for a long innings. Taking care of one's health amounts to reducing downtime, increasing productivity and ability to derive pleasure from work in the truest sense. The consequence of any work ultimately is – joy. One should be able to derive that and for this reason should remain ailment-free.

I have absolutely no intention to either advice in this book or give suggestions. I only intend to share with you whatever I have experienced in so many years. Many will certainly benefit from this. And I will be happy if it happens so. If possible, do let me know your experience about the impact of this book. I will be delighted with that. In conclusion, I feel and wish that business culture should flourish in our country. If you have liked this endeavor of mine or felt nice about it, I humbly appeal to you to give this book to others to read. I shall await your e-mail, SMS, letter.

—Dr. Suresh Haware
B.Sc. Tech. Nuclear Scientist, Ph.D.
416, Vardhaman Market, Sector 17,
Vashi, Navi Mumbai, Maharashtra (India) 400705.
e-mail: md@haware.com
Mobile: 98218 63397 (SMS or Whatsapp Only)

Gratitude

I am highly indebted to the readers of my book on this subject in Marathi titled, *Udyog Tumcha, Paisa Dusryacha*. This book has become the bestseller in Marathi. Many youngsters requested me to make it available in English. And hence this book. I did not just translate the book in English, but revised and renewed it based on the readers' experience and valuable feedback received from them. There are number of additions and improvements over the Marathi book. The narration is done keeping in mind the wide readership the book will receive. I express my sincere gratitude to all the readers and well wishers for their suggestions and encouragement. Thanks are due to my entire Haware family viz. Nalini, Amit, Richa, Amar, Ishaanee and the little master Aryan for their inputs and additions and Vishwarath Nair for his valuable help.

Contents

1

Business without Money

"Capital isn't scarce. Vision is."

—**Sam Walton,** CEO of Wal-Mart

You must have observed many a time that, often whenever anyone is in a lot of problems, there are many people forthcoming with advice. But when we ourselves are confronted with such a situation then only we are stunned. Today, I am not going to give you any advice. I will give you a new perspective. I want you to understand this properly.

Many people, rather all people think that a lot of money is required to do business. Many also feel that if their father was rich, they too would have done business only. I wish to tell you out of experience that feeling in both these ways are wrong. Today there are many millionaires and billionaires in society. They have money lying idle and some of them do not even know what to do with it. And also there are people with lot of business ideas but no money with them. These two people are complimentary to each other. So out of experience I wish to tell you a fact that, no money is required to do business. Business has to be done with others' money. That means, the business can be done without using your money or without your having money. Therefore, one has to be attentive to this new perspective. Along with this, the meaning of others' money and how this can be obtained for your business should be understood. Every page in this book has presented this theme and stated the policy related to it.

So now, let us understand the meaning of 'Others' money'. There are many people around us, among relatives, neighbours or friends' circle, who may not have a lot of money but do have some little money. If you present your project to them and they find it profitable, they could invest in your business. Otherwise their money is deposited in their bank in fixed deposits. They get regular interest on this. It is a fact that the interest is less. But they feel it is safe to keep them deposited in a bank. If they find the same security in investing in your business they will definitely approach you. Now this security should reflect in your conversations, conduct and your day-to-day performance. Along with this, you can also assure them in writing, i.e. promissory notes, memorandum of understanding, agreement, contract, affidavit and other means. You can decide the share of profits that they will get. Suppose, you have decided on a 50:50 formula, which is normally the case, then you should share the profits equally. They get their return on investment and you get paid for your effort. You should be able to convince them that this return on investment is substantially more than the interest offered by the banks. That way you easily get an investor. And if this really happens at the very first instance, then you can be sure that you have got your investor. Apart from this, he will spread word of profits made from this investment to their network and advertise your business and business capabilities.

Thereby enabling you to attract more investment and increase capital for business. This situation may appear very easy to read, but is very difficult to practically implement. You will have to put your entire effort and all your strengths at stake. You have to be ever alert. You have to keep round the clock vigil on everything. You have to extract work from the people with you, with love. In short, this is a big test in your life. If you pass in this and further behave in the same manner, then you can be sure that you have become a businessman and you have found the formula to grow big. However, if you err in this and exhibit negligence saying, "it's okay, what do I have to lose?" And think that anyway the money belongs to somebody else and if your project fails, causing loss to your investor, then be sure your chance of becoming a businessman has ended forever. Because, your investor will not keep mum. He will then inform tens of people and discredit you. No one will look to invest with you in future. Your credibility in the market will end. Hence, it is very essential to take great care in your first venture. And if it is a small one, it will be within your control. For, we too do not have a perfect estimate of our capabilities in the beginning. Therefore, venture out after taking all precautions and ensuring that it will not fail. This is not very difficult. And it is no rocket science either. It is a business deal and this will help enhance your business acumen and knowledge.

Let us understand this point with a small example. A certain person wants to do business of selling crackers, he has no money with him and yet he wants to do business. He should get an investor from nearby his place itself, may be a neighbor, a relative, a friend and so on and buy the crackers. He should sell them and after returning the investment, he should give 50% of the profits and 50% of the balance crackers to the investor. He has now become a businessman. It is so simple. There are many such small businesses, e.g. Diwali delicacies, decorative items, incense sticks, candles, etc. Do not think that these are very small things. Just want to tell you that the founders of P&G, Procter and Gamble, started their business with the selling of candles only. Now it's a multi national company.

One more thing is put to test in all those deals and that is integrity. If you resort to a bit of unfair means, you will certainly profit a little more. For you alone have an estimate of your profit. The investor does not know this. But there is the threat of foul means becoming a habit. You do not realize when this increases, you are unable to go far and last longer. Hence, you should take utmost care to prevent even a fraction of unfair practices creeping into your dealing, behavior and character. Remember the saying, "Shortcut will cut you short."

Booking Advance

Let us understand another important issue here. Just as you managed to get the investors' money, you can also get it from the customer. If you get advance booking for your goods and services, collect an advance of 10-20 per cent, the customer's money can meet your capital need. Many a time, customers are given discounts for payments made for booking in advance, let us say a house, book or any other thing. Customers too benefit from this. Customers are happily willing to pay advance if they are convinced that the discount amount is more than the interest that they can get from the bank. Capital is raised in the above two ways in several businesses. Here too, it is the test of your performance. Your credibility increases and this leads to the growth of the business, if you deal as you have agreed upon and provide the decided goods or services at the decided price. Many booksellers advertise a book even before it is printed and raise capital in the form of advance registration. Computer services and maintenance contracts are done this way with advance payment. Infrastructure contracts of the government are tendered and the successful bidders are given a percentage of the whole amount as mobilization advance. Thus, you can take advance amount to raise capital for your goods or services.

Get Early, Pay Later

You can provide the required capital for business by following the policy of "Recover Early, Pay Later." Now while doing business you have to pay the price to raw materials suppliers, the contractor and service providers. Similarly you have to recover costs from your customers. Then alone the businessman gets several goods and services on credit. Some payments are made as per the credit terms of the agreement entered into while buying the goods, in say 7 days, 15 or 30 days. The other significant reason to avail credit period is to be able to return the goods, if defective goods are supplied. Since you have not paid for them, there is nothing binding on you and the supplier takes back the bad goods supplied and sends good materials. It is always better to sell goods or services and recover the payments earlier. This will help in easy control of the business. Thus, when you recover from the customer immediately and as agreed, you have to pay the supplier much later, then you get to use the capital in the meantime. Let us understand this with a small example. Suppose that the cost of the daily requirement of raw material is ₹ 1 lakh and your daily income is ₹ 1 lakh, then in this situation there is no balance left with you. But if you have an agreement to pay for the goods, materials and services after seven days and collect receivable payments immediately from the customers then you will always have ₹ 7 lakh liquid capital with you. And if you have the payment credit of 30 days then you will have a liquid capital of ₹ 30 lakhs. Thus, you have the suppliers' money serving your business! Here also your credibility matters. If the supplier gets payment on the agreed date, then he will continue supplying you regularly. Not merely these, in course of time he will also reduce rates and extend the credit period further. Sometimes, supplier firms announce incentive schemes and you get additional benefit of that too.

HNI and NRI

Now you must understand the terms HNI and NRI. High Net worth Individuals (HNI) are those citizens who have a lot of money. They spend their life in money management only. Their objective is to invest and earn more money. When your business grows and you need big investment, then it will be in your interest to approach HNIs. They scrutinize the business and observe minute details. They have their own lawyer and chartered accountant. They study the legality and possibilities of risks and profits very minutely. They bargain for share of profits. They appoint an observer on your business.

But once they are convinced and become confident about your business and your way of doing business, then there will be no need to worry about capital. There is a big chain (network) of such HNIs. They circulate their money among each other. Some people come together and raise capital on a very large scale too. HNIs stay in India and NRIs (Non-Resident Indian) stay abroad. They too have such a network in their respective nations. In countries in America – Europe bank deposits earn just 1-2 per cent annual interest, or nothing. Hence, all these NRIs are keen to invest in India. Now it is indeed a task to rope in a network of such NRIs. You have to reach them through contacts. They do not expect huge returns. But they need the facility to withdraw their investment whenever they need that is facility to divest on demand. Several such groups are active in India. Thus, the money of the NRIs too can meet the capital needs of your business. So far we have discussed individual capital only. Let us now look at organized capital for the start-ups.

Start Up Business

Today banks are flushed with huge idle funds. The same situation prevails all over the nation. Hence, banks have reduced interest rate on deposits. The number of people seeking loan from banks far out-number those wanting to deposit money. For, banks pay interest to the depositors and they become the takers. The loan takers give revenue to the banks, in the form of interest, so they are the givers. It is always the givers who reign. In such a situation, it is a loss for the banks, if the money lies idle. Hence, banks are in search of worthy businessmen. Even from the point of view of the businessmen, loan from banks is any day better, as they take it after due investigation of the legal aspects. The bank legally verifies the documents of the business. Hence, there is little risk of being cheated. And also the banks' interest rate is less than that of loan from private individuals or organizations. Only you should have the patience to complete their complicated process and show them the transparency they require. Banks can provide capital for small and big businesses. For start-ups, to start a small business, if you have some property, then the banks can mortgage it too and provide a loan. Through Mudra Bank, one can easily get the loan to start up a new business. Even all the leading banks have been informed by the Central Government to make available the initial funds for the start-ups.

Partnerships

Even partnership is a good and trustworthy method to raise capital. A partnership can be forged with the investors' capital and your effort, concept, and skill. It can be registered with the government. It then assumes a legal, constitutional identity. There are many people willing to become such partners. They feel secure in such partnerships as they get ownership rights too in business. You can take more than one such partner. After the firm grows big you can make it a private limited company and then a public limited company. That means you accommodate more and more persons as stakeholders in your company by reducing your share in the company's stake. Public limited companies can register themselves in the share market and can raise capital from the people. There are thousands of such companies in existence today. Most of the big companies are of this type. Thus, the investors' money is invested in these companies and huge businesses are functioning on investors' money.

Debt-Equity Route

Today there are several private companies in the market willing to provide capital. They supply capital in two ways – one is in the form of loans (debt) and the other is private partnership (private equity). Interest has to be paid on capital borrowed in the form of loan. This rate of interest is more than the bank's rate of interest. But in businesses, where the risk factor is high, capital is seen to be raised in this way. Also private equity is another popular source. They need not be returned too. In lieu of that they have to be made a partner in the business. Here too where the risk factor is more, the share of the partner is proportionately larger.

Joint Venture

Joint venture is also another way to raise capital or doing business. In this, suppose the land is your own and you take a JV partner, then this partner spends for everything, from getting all permissions to constructing the houses. The product, which houses or money (profits), is distributed as agreed upon. Then each one can sell their respective products. Some may sell early, some later, some cheaper, some costlier. It is their respective independent decision.

FDI and FII

Now the meaning of FDI and FII should be understood. Foreign direct investment (FDI) means direct investment from abroad. Foreign Institutional investor (FII) means investment from institutions abroad. All this money comes from fcreign countries. The Indian Government controls all those investments. These investments are made in huge amounts and are useful for mega projects.

Therefore, you must now be convinced that business means indulging with others' investments. So those who want to do business or expand their existing business should not be worried about capital, i.e. money at all. They should be firm to utilize others' investment and get to work. These alone are not enough here. I give maximum credence to trustworthiness. Rather, in my opinion "Trust indeed is the lifeline of business." Once you earn the trust, all other things do follow. But the biggest base that trust rests upon is honesty. I feel like admitting that these days honesty is observed to be neglected a bit. The extreme of this can be seen in some places in the government service. That means once a government institution is established to enhance business and an honest person is appointed its chief, unfortunately one observes that, "the meaning he takes of honesty is, you should do nothing."

People are afraid of failures and committing mistakes. I think, you should not be. If you do something, may be mistakes may take place. It does not mean that to avoid mistakes, you should do nothing. According to me, this is wrong. Doing work is the primary need. Wherever you are, there is no alternative to doing work. Many believe that business cannot be done without indulging in unfair means. But this is false. You should have faith that business can be done and also expanded by honesty and fair means. If this is imbibed in the mind of all businessmen and aspiring businessmen, then there certainly will be a great deal of resultant benefits to the society. We should have faith that business can be done honestly.

Crowd Funding

Crowd funding is a recently generated new way of raising funds by asking a large number of people to lend or invest a small amount of money. With the increasing usage of Internet and social media platforms, a new platform for fund raising has been created in the form of crowd funding. The ease of accessing and sharing information allows people to share their ideas and products with the world at large. Crowd funding makes use of the easy accessibility of vast networks of family, friends, colleagues, and like-minded individuals through social media websites like Facebook, Twitter, Whatsapp and LinkedIn to promote new businesses and attract investors. The platform allows people to comment, criticise, and share their views on the innovations and creations of other people. It also allows people to demonstrate their ideas, products or services to people, who in turn can invest in the ideas that interest them. Crowd funding is used at the first stage of product life cycle of the company. This is when the new product is promoted. Crowd funding was majorly used for new products, rather than services, when it first started. This is because the investors generally get the early stage prototype of the product in return of their investment. But with the increasing acceptance of crowd funding as a model for raising substantial investments, services, and non-tangible products have also started using this platform for their capital requirements. In a way, it is like pre-selling a product. Crowd funding is also majorly used for raising smaller ticket size loans. Large private equity and venture funds usually have a minimum ticket size which is still very large for an SME as their cost of operations are higher. Crowd funding frees entrepreneurs from having to raise unnecessarily large amount of investment just because the large investors have a minimum investment limit.

Crowd funding is also of different types – it can be donation crowd funding, where the funders fund to make a good idea come alive, but do not expect anything in return. Another type of crowd funding is reward crowd funding, where the funders are rewarded with something. People invest based on the utility of the product or service, or based on the vision for the product that has been showcased by the inventor. In return, people either get part equity in the company, like in any other private equity investment. Sometimes, they also get early stage prototypes of the products that are being developed, making them the early adapters of technology and innovation. Some crowd funding is also a form of debt, where the lenders get their money back with interest.

Venture Capital

Venture capital (VC) is a form of private equity where the venture capital fund invests in the early stage of growth of a company. In return for the investment, the venture capitalist usually takes a large equity in the company. As the VC fund is an equity partner, it is in their interest to grow the company they invest in. Typically, VCs take board membership in the investee companies, along with guiding and training the management on ways to grow their businesses. They also provide their expertise of the industry and market and provide access to their distribution network and contacts in various other companies. As the VCs get involved in activities of the investee company, most VC funds have specific industry verticals they invest in. They also usually aim to have companies whose businesses can be aligned with each other, so that they can help each other grow. As VCs are involved in early stage of the company, they usually look for businesses with high growth potential that can generate significant returns. As a result, most of the investments are in new and innovative technologies or products that have the potential to grow. Very often, the investee companies are at such an early stage of growth that no bank would lend to them. They do not have any property or huge credit line available. But they are at a stage where they can launch their product or service when the funding becomes available. This is another characteristic of the VC. A VC does not invest in the first stage or the start of the company. That is usually covered by angel investors, who are another type of private equity investors. The VC invests when the company has already finalized its plan, has some operations, maybe has developed a prototype of a new product, and need funding to take it to manufacturing and generate revenues. VCs look to grow their investee companies to a stage where they can recuperate their investments by either taking the company public through an IPO, or by selling the company to another large company from which the investee company is a strategic fit, or by selling their stake to another bigger private equity firm, which can further grow the company. As VC invests in early stage, the risk that the VC bears is large. In return for this large risk, the VC seeks a higher equity stake in the company.

By now, you must have got fair idea of the concept that money cannot be the starting point of the business. It is the business idea that is the starting point. And also that having no money cannot hold you from doing business. In fact, you do not need your money to do the business. It has to be necessarily done by using other's money. It is amply available around you, only you need to hone up your skills to lay hands on that through fair and legitimate business means.

"Business is a Journey, Not a Destination."

□

2

Start With What You Have

"Creative skills and gainful productive work alone can cure India of her poverty."

—Shantanurao Kirloskar

When it is difficult to smile, let us meet and greet each other with a smile. Alexandria Skiathitis said "As you travel on life's way, with its many ups and downs, remember it's quite true to say one smile is worth a dozen frowns." In reality, most of us spend a lifetime finding the truth in this statement. Each one of us searches for ways on how to live life. There is no question of those whose living is bliss. But those who want to progress and find bliss in bringing joy to others' life, have to find some formula to live life as a song. According to me, business is the best path for achieving this. I do not think there is any other active means as 'businesses' to fulfill your dreams. Not only knowledge and prosperity thrive at the homes of such businesses, but you also can get the satisfaction of fulfilling your duty to your family, society, nation, and the wide global world.

It is the kind of satisfaction that embraced Navalmal Firodia. The whole family of Navalmal Firodia, who was born in Ahmednagar district of Maharashtra (India), was full of political and social ideologies. In the pre-independence days, Navalmal Firodia plunged himself into the freedom movement. Even after getting freedom, the urge to do something for the society, the country, would not allow him to be in peace. You have to create new wealth if you want your country to progress and prosper. He proposed in his mind that employment would be generated from that, the nation's productivity would increase and that would enhance national revenue and the nation will march forward in the path of development. From his contribution to the freedom movement, he had developed the strong attitude, of moving forward with determination once a decision was taken.

With the efforts of Navalmal and Hastimal and co-operation of Bajaj, the world famous successful venture of 'Bajaj Tempo' was started from a cattle pond of buffaloes in Goregaon, Mumbai. It is important to start anything. Where it starts is not significant. If the objective is decided and the methods fair, then success is certain, no matter where and how you start.

Chatrapati Shivaji Maharaj scripted the saga of freedom with a handful of *mavalas* (devoted soldiers) when he was only sixteen years of age. With that modest initiative, he attained Self-Rule (Independence). With just five child *swayamsevaks* (volunteers), Dr. Hedgewar started the now gigantic organization, viz. Rashtriya Swayamsevak Sangh in a dilapidated mansion in Nagpur.

Anna Bedekar, who fought odds at every step, set up Bedekar pickles that have conquered taste buds worldwide, with the first lot of 200 lemons that he purchased from the market. Dahanukar, the industrialist, came to Mumbai with just ₹ 5/- in his pocket. His relative dispossessed him of his drinking water vessel too. "I will drink water from a vessel made of dry leaves, but I will achieve something on my own", he determined. He could carve a new world. Somebody has rightly stated that all these achievers were bound by one ideology, which was –

Start from where you are,
Start with what you have,
Do something of it and
Never be satisfied.

The above four lines are the beginning of a new world or the assurance of accomplishing that world. No one can do anything without deciding in his mind on what to do. And nothing will happen if you keep waiting for an auspicious moment after you have firmly decided in your mind to do something. A Sanskrit verse makes a comprehensive description of such a situation, which states

Udhyamenahi Sidhyanti,
Karyani Na Manorathaiy,
Na Hi Suptasya Sinhasya
Pravishanti Mukhe Mrugaha.

Meaning – the lion has to strive and hunt for food himself. The deer will not, on its own, enter the sleeping lion's mouth.

Thus, by doing work alone; through business you can fulfill your desires. The author of this verse has summed up the essence of the whole business world. What better advice can there be to good people, than to always remain in a working mode. Renowned author and motivator Shiv Khera has cited a very good example in his book *You can Win*. The seller of gas balloons releases various gas balloons into the sky. At that time a small boy standing beside him asks him, "will a black colored balloon fly in the sky?" "And will the red colored also fly?" On that the seller very casually states, "son, these balloons do not fly due to their color. They fly due to what is (the gas) filled in them."

Your approach to life is decided by the urge fastened in your mind. Your life philosophy is decided by this urge. Business is action, this is what is generally believed. And apparently this is true too. But after some thought you will realize that business is not action but a state of mind (attitude, tendency, mentality). In any business, action is the second step. Before any action, business should be imprinted in your mind. This will render your state of mind suitable to business. Some people are gifted with this attitude in their genes. They do not have to endeavor much for this. Just as the renowned vocalist Kumar Gandharva was enthused to strike one great melody after the other, so also business ideas flow by itself from an individual's mind. The enthusiasm or obsession with any such ideas, are what I term as the tendency suited to business. A person in this state of mind can never relax. He will venture out of his routine state and automatically develop the boldness to accept new challenges, and this happens due to such a state of mind that achieves through strife.

The example of Sheth Walchand Hirachand can be aptly cited. He belonged to an era when Maharashtra, rather the whole of India, was not well aware about the industrial sector. He was obsessed with the business mentality. Walchand, born in a not very big town of

Sholapur, had a different frame of mind. He lost his two elder brothers suddenly, when his education was on. Because of this, everybody expected Walchand to take up the traditional business of the family. Walchand entered business thus, but he was obsessed with doing something new. He undertook the contract of constructing a railway line from Yedshi to Tadhval in Maharashtra, at the age of 22. Following this, he started bagging several railway contracts. He set up projects to manufacture trains, ships, cars, and aeroplanes. He brought the sugar industry and manufacture of equipments business to prosperity. He ventured into so many businesses that, it will be easier to list the industries that Walchand did not attempt. He constantly travelled and from the experiences of the many people he met during his journey, he was inspired by new ideas. If you take note of the innumerable obstacles in the pre-independence days, you will realize that all this would not have been possible without untiring willpower.

The viewpoint of a businessman is absolutely different. People in every sector develop a viewpoint out of their experience. Policemen instantly recognize a pickpocketer in a crowd on the streets. A seasoned journalist sniffs news instantly. Similarly, a businessman instantly understands where a business opportunity lies. These words of veteran industrialist late Shantanurao Kirloskar are very significant – "We Kirloskars do not bring our products to a market where the markets are available. We always search for and create new markets." The Kirloskar Group specially excelled in discovering such markets and conquering them with their hard work. They had the business tendency, mental obsession, and the businessman's viewpoint. As the Kirloskar Group stabilized in industry, their scope of work too started widening. The number of guests in the Pune office started growing very much. They included prominent people from India and abroad. The lodging and boarding arrangement, of the guests had to be done always. This involved expenses, but for the employees the daily booking of rooms in different hotels was becoming very strenuous. One day a thought came to Shantanurao's mind – "Everyday we have to arrange the guests' stay. What if we started a hotel of our own?" This began with a thought and gradually came into fruition. Thus, the five-star hotel 'Blue Diamond' project took shape. He asked his wife, Yamunatai, to run this project. This is called the foresight for a business opportunity.

One more side of the special characteristics of a businessman is his foresight and readiness for untiring effort. Ordinary people see the businessman's money, bungalow, cars, and air travels. But they do not see his hard work. They have to completely study their field of activity. They have to understand the capacity and mental inclination of people around them. They have to assess in their mind the plan for the coming 30-40 years and make their moves. They should have the view to think of many issues completely. Most important of all they have to take flawless spot decisions. They have to accomplish the right timing to grab any opportunity. People thinking only of their own growth cannot become a successful businessman. If they entertain only that limited thought then they become narrow-minded. Such people cannot progress beyond a particular limit. They have to think in a broader sense of the good of the society at large along with their own growth. In a way, they can succeed if they link their individual progress with the welfare of the society.

The founder president of Bharatiya Mazdoor Sangh late Dattopant Tengadi used to convincingly present his point, 'Individual to Totality' in his speeches. In the Indian school of thought, the individual, family, village, state, and nation are all connected to each other. Also going beyond the nation, they are connected globally. That is why you prominently come across the concept of 'Vasudhaiva Kutumbakam' or welfare of the world, in Indian philosophy. Businessmen too cannot think about development in isolation. They have to link individual development to the development of the family, the development of the family to the development of the village, the development of the village to the development of the nation and the development of the nation to the welfare of the globe. Those who can link so, alone can succeed in the true sense. Thus, businessmen cannot de-link themselves from global welfare. However, development can never be of one individual. It can sustain and last only if it happens to everyone.

Finally, it is important that the businessman is a leader. Leadership qualities are essential to become a successful businessman. He has to combat on four fronts at the same time – personal, family, social, and professional. Without having imbibed leadership qualities, he cannot do this. Several people fight on one or two of these fronts. Businessmen have to fight on all the four fronts at the same time.

Field Marshall Manekshaw has described 'leadership' very well. His description applies not merely to military leadership, but to leadership in all fields. Manekshaw always mentioned a sentence of Confucius, the Chinese philosopher – "Every great man prominently has three special qualities. Being meritorious he has no worries, being clever he is not confused, being courageous he is fearless." These three qualities are applicable to people wanting to lead in the world of business too. Businessmen have to confront challenges with the limited resources at their disposal. Only such well-endowed and capable leadership can build the world of business. In a way, it is like the creation of a new world by the likes of Vishwakarma. It will certainly be worthwhile to search for historical links of such concepts.

"Your capacity varies according to the challenges you accept."

□

3

Historical Roots

"Anyone who stops learning is aged; whether at twenty or eighty. Anyone, who keeps learning, stays young."

—Henry Ford

It is said that the concept of leadership takes shape where more than one people gather together. Business leadership is considered to be a very active-leadership. Western thinkers believe that Socrates the Greek philosopher first coined the concept of leadership. But this is not true. The concept of leadership is very ancient, almost as old as the advent of human civilization. Indian civilization is the most ancient civilization in the world. The concept of leadership took shape from the beginning of this civilization. From this concept, the generation of finance was created and from that came business. Our epic *Mahabharat* is, in a way, part of the struggle for leadership. Meera Uberai has very well written the book titled, *Leadership Secrets from the Mahabharat*. It can be said that every character in the *Mahabharat* was obsessed with the concept of leadership. In the various episodes of the *Mahabharat*, the many sides of social life have been brought out in realistic detail.

There is also a wide discussion on the subject of financial sector in it. The discussion of all three issues – finance, business, wealth, is not restricted to the *Mahabharat* alone, but is also in the ancient Upanishads. The *rishis* had realized the unassailable significance of finance and wealth in the development of human life. Vedic thought does not subscribe to the avoidance of wealth and the rich. Vedic *rishis* totally reject the pessimistic view – 'Everything is void', meaning zero – everything is momentary. The economics that they adhere to is the science that is useful for human development in society. The wealth that they appeal for demolishes sorrow, poverty, and misery and shapes life. This wealth is created from leadership. Earlier leadership and wealth were jointly thought about. Then an independent group of wealth creators was established (Ref-Srisukta.). You are all aware of the philosopher Kautilya alias Arya Chanakya who successfully put Indian philosophy to use in practical dealing. Chanakya not only avenged the insult he was subjected to with assistance from Chandragupta, but also properly stabilized the social life and financial health of the kingdom. Chanakya has given a very clear and exhaustive and lucid analysis of the generation and distribution of wealth. It is a reality that even today we cannot move forward by ignoring his economics. Chanakya formulated rules and policy after studying the inter-relationship of governments, wealth and society, which will guide us for years to come. The situation that prevailed in the Magadh kingdom, is more or less with little variance, the same today. Dr. Pawan Varma, in his book, *Chanakya's New Manifesto to Resolve the Crisis in India*, in a well-researched analysis stated how Chanakya's rules and philosophy are therefore relevant even today. He has stressed a sentence from Chanakya's economics, "The root of wealth is economic activity. In absence of fruitful activity, both current prosperity and future growth are in danger of destruction." From the above sentence, you can imagine what in-depth thought Chankya gave to wealth, finance, and business. Economic activity is needed for nation building and harmonizing social life and if it is not there then the nation will suffer material loss and sink to lowest levels of degradation. Chanakya presented the basic philosophy itself of modern economics. Chanakya's theme stressed that economic thought should be about inclusive welfare of the whole society. Even in the earlier mentioned book of Meera Uberai *Leadership Secrets from the Mahabharat* the very same point is mentioned. A king who is mindful only of the means of acquiring profit never succeeds in acquiring either merit or wealth, she has mentioned this statement in the *Mahabharat*. The *Mahabharat* has given the basic mantra (teaching) that the State should exist for the welfare of the people alone and from public service alone the State's basic development will be done. Every word of this principle, laid down by the author of the *Mahabharat* and Chanakya for the nation, is applicable in the present times to business also. Even though the State and business are two different entities, the underlying principle or spirit being the same, the ancient principle of wealth from business, employment from wealth and social welfare from employment continues to be applicable in all ways, even today. May it be the issues of the economic system, social welfare or management, most of its' principles have been written by Chanakya only. For several centuries, India's rulers followed the traditions based on these principles alone.

When Chatrapati Shivaji Maharaj established the Hindvi Swaraj, his politics was then linked with fiscal policy and the concept of a welfare state was the very foundation. You can find mention of this, many a time, in the character of Shivaji Maharaj. Shivaji Maharaj has stated, "The businessmen are the decoration of the State and the ruler". Hence, the businessmen should be respected and keeping them satisfied, trade of all kinds of commodities should be conducted in the state. The businessmen that Shivaji Maharaj envisaged were the main financial backbone of those times. Wealth is toyed around through them. This means that when the Maharaj called for taking care of the businessmen he had a broader fiscal philosophy and ultimately Maharaj had public welfare alone in mind. Shri Golawalkar Guruji has supported the same economic policies for public welfare. In an interview to renowned journalist Jilani, Guruji had stated that the network of small industries and cottage industries should spread everywhere. These small industries should supply goods to big industrial centers. Spare parts can be manufactured at various places and they can be assembled in the big industries. The main objective should be to generate maximum employment and to distribute financial wealth to the maximum number of people. Accordingly, the proportion of economic planning, industrialization, and technology orientation should be decided. Economic policy should be welfare oriented. But Guruji stated that nothing but the enhancement of trade alone could achieve that. He firmly believed that if the growth of business was linked to discipline, hard work, and national pride, then the fortune of any nation can turn around like Japan and Germany. The examples of Japan and Germany in this context are astonishing. Both these countries were reduced to ashes in World War II. But merely on the strength of national pride, strict discipline, and untiring hard work, these countries re-built their nation. Japanese companies like Toyota and Sony shook the mighty industrial sector of the American empire. They scaled new heights in manufacturing; improved management techniques and started new marketing methods. Businessmen in these countries improved the situation of the nations that came to the brink of bankruptcy. They not only improved the situation, but also placed their nation in the top rung of nations. But this influence lasted for some years after independence. Gradually, the two vices, corruption and laziness, started devouring India. Fairness and truthfulness were not valued. The reason being *Swadesh* (nation) and *Swabhiman* (self-esteem) were considered insignificant. Without the foundation of national pride and patriotism, money alone came to be considered 'everything' in life. From this grew corruption, a vicious cycle of power from corruption and corruption from power got into motion. A nation moving fast towards progress, India was stalled mid-way. China started the journey with us around same time and look, where they have reached. In manufacturing and exports, China outpaced India several times. The selfishness in India touched the extremes. All failures were attributed to particular groups of rival or opposed thinking or foreigners. Assuming that 'today is our day', everyone started filling his or her own coffers. Only a burning national policy based on patriotism can pull the nation out of this quagmire. Business has a huge role to play in this national *yagna* (movement), as, after agriculture, business is the biggest creator of wealth in our country. The two biggest responsibilities of the nation's progress and development rest on the shoulders of the business sector. The nation's progress and development depends on the wealth created by business. From this alone employment is generated for the people. For the well-being of the nation, the business sector should function well and the trade should be good. Businessmen should also be equally responsible for the proper functioning of the business, just as the government and the society should be. Therefore, the loyalty of businessmen, their integrity, professional skills, promptness, readiness to work hard, and professional merit are very significant. In one way, these qualities can change the nation's profile. Hence, a comprehensive thought should be given to the business sector, people in business, the inherent opportunities, possibility of sudden threats or risks and the challenges therein. Though there may not be a specific science on how to create wealth from business, how to make it grow and achieve the progress of the nation and ultimately social welfare, yet much can be achieved through studies and experience. Can all these be achieved through efforts? Like all other arts, business too is divine art and destiny has a major role to play in it, according to certain traditional school of thought. Hence, many people are apprehensive at the very mention of the word 'business'. There is nothing like this. Many things are achieved with hard work. Industrialists and businessmen like Tata, Ambani, Mahindras, Godrej, Kirloskar, Shirke, Bajaj, Bedekar, etc. were created in this very world. Once a businessman begins chasing wealth, then competition and progress alone become his objectives, and to expand his empire and sustain it, he can go to any extent. Several large companies in America have grown to monstrous proportions because of this competition and ambition.

From this bloody competition, the world steers to destruction instead of development. To avoid this, it should be seen as to how people inspired by positive emotions turn to the business field and to how these people succeed in business. We shall delve on this in the following chapters.

"Values and ethics are the foundations on which the structure of success stands."

□

4

Commencement of Work

"At the end of the day, you can decide whether you want to be an employee with a great attendance record, getting promoted to ever better titles and working on interesting projects, or whether you want to attempt to do something spectacular. This be and do should be a question you never stop asking yourself for the next 20 years and beyond."

—**Steve Blank,** Serial Entrepreneur

We do every work twice. First we decide and do it in mind and then in reality. All work first commences in the mind. The very urge to do the work could be a turning point in one's life, and continuing to do the work, confronting several difficulties and obstacles, will certainly yield success. The above three steps are perfectly applicable to any business. That means any decision to undertake a new work has to be taken by you in the mind. Thus, without preparing your mindset, you cannot venture ahead a single step. Your first step after your mind is set is the turning point in your life. To get hold of this turning point, your mindset has to be positive. The mind should always be hopeful. Only those who believe that "a glass is neither half full nor half empty, it is always full, half with water and half with air," can make something of their life.

Achyut Godbole has given a good example in his book, *The Boardroom*. A big shoes manufacturing company in Japan sent two marketing officials to a remote, backward region in South Africa for sales promotion. Nobody used shoes or chappals in that region. One of the sales executives got frustrated and informed the company the very next day that "nobody uses shoes, chappals here. It is not a practice here. Hence, there is no use being here. When should I come back?" The other sales executive informed the company, "No one has shoes, chappals here. There is a lot of opportunity for us here. Hence, dispatch a thousand pairs of shoes, chappals."

The above viewpoint is a must, prior to commencing any work. People should have this kind of temperament to enter the world of business, which has a potential to change the face of the whole nation. Adam Smith, the renowned economist had titled his book on economics as *Wealth of Nations*. In one way, any small experiment is a step taken with a view to create wealth. In that lies the prosperity of the individual or family, but ultimately it becomes the subject of the nation's development and wide reaching social welfare. Hence, the path of business alone, in a true sense, is the path to the progress of the nation.

Though this path may lure many and be lavish, it certainly is not an easy one. Renowned industrialist and a father figure of the business world in Maharashtra, Shantanurao Kirloskar has given the title *Cactus and Roses* to his autobiography. Meaning, there certainly are roses on this path, but those wanting to tread this path should be prepared for the cactus too. He has stated this in the very title of his autobiography. He intends to state that all those wanting to tread this path should not enter this field in a dreamy way, a world of dreamy imagination. These are the words of experience of an industrialist who initially started his business with ₹ 3 lakh and grew his business to ₹ 5000 crores. Shantanurao Kirloskar has stated in this very book, "my fifty years claim that creative skill and gainful productive work alone can cure India of her poverty". Business is the highway to pull the nation out of the depths of poverty, stated Kirloskar. He used to say that this path should be tried by scores of youth. He proved this to the society by setting an ideal example of his life.

Most of the famous businessmen in the world have certainly experienced this cactus in the initial period of their work. Promoters of many big companies have established their business from zero (nothing). They made many big mistakes, faced many setbacks, bore unbearable loss, but they never lost courage. Just as the poet Harivanshrai Bachhan states, "Those who show courage never fail," as if those words were penned for them only.

The founder of Coca-Cola that reigned over the whole world is an ideal example of this. Coca-Cola has today given an identity to a mighty nation like America. Coca-Cola sells crores of bottles every day. It is known as the only drink available in every country in the world. The President of America Eisenhower had himself advertised this drink. The annual turnover of Coca-Cola some years ago was about US $50 billion. A company, that established such a huge kingdom, had a very rickety, rough beginning. When the founder of the company, Asa Candler, started the company, he barely managed to sell

10-12 bottles per day. His first year's earning was a mere $50. With great effort and innovative ideas, the founder of the company linked the product to America's national pride and gradually, over a period of time the Coca-Cola empire spread worldwide. This one company produced over 250 products.

Even in India, there are many examples that will testify this very experience. Babasaheb Dahanukar, the man behind the growth of the rising graph of the Dahanukar Group left for Mumbai to put his destiny to test. While leaving his father gave him a vessel for drinking water, which his relative took away from him. "I will not be cowed down or look back. I will drink water from a vessel made of dry leaves," stating so, he left. He had just ₹ 5 with him. He came to Mumbai and struggled. He met Lokmanya Tilak sometime, who told him, "Youngsters like you should do business." Those words of Lokmanya kept ringing in his ears. Those inspiring words became a turning point in his life. Babasaheb turned to business. There were obstacles, but now there was the determination to surmount those obstacles. A very hard struggle commenced. And Dahanukar Industries Group came into being.

Here I feel, it is essential to understand clearly as to what is struggle. Let us take a small example.

Once a teacher was narrating the story of the birth of butterflies. He decided to narrate it with practical demonstration. He kept a decorated table in the center of the class and placed a butterfly egg on it. Stating that the butterfly will soon be born and asking the students to practically watch the same, he went out of the classroom for sometime. While going out he instructed all the students not to touch the egg at all. In a short while the movement of the egg commenced. It cracked a bit and the butterfly began to struggle to come out of the shell. That was the butterfly's struggle. One student felt pity thinking that the butterfly must be in great pain and undergoing great difficulty, and out of compassion he broke the shell cover and very carefully pulled the butterfly out. But the butterfly died instantly.

The teacher understood the whole thing. Hence, he said, "From the effort, the struggle to come out of the hard shell, the butterfly was to get its strength. Its wings would be strengthened with that struggle. With that strength it was to fly. But out of compassion you denied it the strength and it fell dead."

Therefore, do not be afraid of struggle. You will gain strength from the struggle to start business. And remember, everyone has to struggle so. And that has to be endured yourself. And you alone have to undergo the struggle. Otherwise you will not acquire the required strength.

This then is the saga of commencement of work. This is not for those who fall back stating that nothing is in our hands. This is for those who consider that even if nothing is in our hands, yet it is our good fortune that we have in our hands at least. If not in our hands, it is in others' hands. Considering those too as our own, link them to your business and then you will realize that without money, nothing is hindered and merely with money, nothing is done. You have to have the attitude, temperament, and mindset for business. There was a plaque put up in a church – "I used to moan that I had no chappals on my feet. I used to complain to God. Instantly my attention was drawn to a man beside me. He did not even have legs." This is a lesson to stop crying over some single issue and to stand up with determination and perform. "Start from where you are; start with what you have," this is the story of those who imbibe this.

The grievance that nothing is in our hands, is in fact is an excuse. Money is required to start a business or industry. But there is no specified figure for that. So when the urge to do business overwhelms the mind, then you can begin some work with whatever money you have at hand. When the mind becomes restless to do business, you start getting different ideas to raise money. Even if many of those ideas tend to fail, one of them will surely succeed.

Money plants: The relatives, friends, neighbors are to be considered as your nearest and dearest money plants. You can depend on them for raising the basically needed seed capital. Try shaking them and you will be surprised to find that really money falls from some of these plants. But to get that money into your pocket, an element of trust plays a vital role. If you establish your trustworthiness, you can be sure to get this money into your pocket.

One of the most important things in this is that mostly you do not have to utilize your money. Utilizing others' money to serve society and fulfill one's duty is the basic principle of doing business. Laxmi (wealth) is very fickle, it is said. Hence, she does not ever stay at one place alone. She is at times with someone and at other times with someone else. Hence, you should think of ways to turn money lying elsewhere towards you by fair means. They alone can raise money, who think thus.

"Raising money from others, creating new wealth from that wealth, earning some profit on that and repaying old debts with that money, raising new structures," is the formula of a successful business.

I have used the word 'by fair means' to raise money. Integrity and fairness are the most essential qualities for long-term success in any field. Without these as the foundation, no structure can stay secure.

Every businessman should bear in mind the principle of trusteeship presented by Mahatma Gandhiji. Business people should be aware of this in whatever task they undertake. If they miss the moral path, then chaos will prevail.

The response you get depends upon how you behave. Hence, while enhancing your business – industry, you should show concern for society. Once you submit your success at the altar of society, you will automatically receive the blessings of society in large measure. Shiv Khera has, in his book, presented a very psychological form of echo. If you say 'I hate you,' the echo will sound 'I hate you.' And if you say,' I love you,' the echo will come 'I love you.' Therefore, if you have love for society in your mind, then you will also receive love from society.

"I don't believe in taking right decisions, I take decisions and make them right."

—**Ratan Tata,** ex-Chairman of Tata Sons

□

5

Building a Business

"I think a simple rule of business is, if you do the things that are easier first, then you can actually make a lot of progress."

—**Mark Zuckerberg,** Chairman and Chief Executive of Facebook

It is said, "If you have to build a ship, then do not tell people to gather logs of wood or do not give any orders. Instead create a yearning in them for the great, vast ocean."

'Well begun is half done,' goes an English saying. But before making this beginning, you should be fully prepared mentally. Once the mind is decided, then no power in the world can defeat you. Harish Bhimani in his portraiture of renowned singer Lata Mangeshkar, has quoted her saying, "When I was eight years old, my father had emphasized that once if you are convinced that what you are doing is right, then fear no one. If you have to fear, fear yourself." These words of Lata Mangeshkar apply to aspiring businessmen in toto. The resolve to accept the challenges of the vast ocean should be somewhere very firm. Once it is firm, then it is not difficult to surmount the mountain of obstacles. One gets the strength automatically. Circumstances teach you. The slogan "We do the difficult things easily. The impossible take some time" of Anuradha Prabhudesai's Lakshya Foundation, an organization that works for soldiers defending our borders, expresses the mental resolve of the soldiers so very well. This sentence that is attributable to the soldiers marching forward facing death is totally applicable to the businessman pushing his boat through the vast ocean of business. He should have the same firm resolve as that in the mind of the soldier in battlefield.

If there is this kind of resolve then in situations that look impossible too, business can be raised from very ordinary work. The example given by Subrato Bagchi, the senior advisory officer of, Mind Tree Company in his book *The Professional* is totally very telling. Rather than an example, it is a story that touches the heart. It is the story of Mahadev of Bengaluru who performs the last rites of unclaimed bodies in a hospital. His mother brought him from a village to Bengaluru. She fed her son and herself, toiling throughout the day. Once she fell sick and got admitted to the hospital. Mahadev began staying with the children there. Mahadev did not even know that his mother died in the sickness. Not knowing the whereabouts of Mahadev, the hospital employees performed the last rites of his mother as an unclaimed body. Mahadev was orphaned. But he refused to return to his village. Somebody in the hospital cared for him and nurtured him. Mahadev did odd jobs in the hospital. One day the police entrusted him the task of performing the last rites of an unclaimed body. Since then he got hooked to this work. He used to get ₹ 200/-for performing the last rites of each unclaimed body. He used to do this work very sincerely, with focus and a sense of belonging, and hence he was always called to perform this task. His work started increasing. Earlier he had a cart. He then purchased a three-wheeler auto-rickshaw. Looking at his service, the petrol pump dealers in the city provided him petrol free of cost. The work kept on increasing. By the time Bagchi's book was published, he had performed the last rites of more than 42000 dead bodies. In a way, this was a very frightening, discouraging, boring, dull service. Looking at the broad nature of the work and the income generated, it could be classified as a social service as an enterprise. A service business that calls for no big chain of capital, marketing, advertising, and employees! The 'service industry' is based merely on the feeling to do something for the society, the preparedness to do hard work and unflinching sincerity.

This means that very little is needed to begin a business. A large amount of capital is not the most indispensable thing for any business. Many great things in the world have been initiated by people, who had no support of money or who lived in abject poverty. They have challenged big businessmen by their sheer hard work, determination, and instinct. They have competed with big multi-national companies. Dhirubhai Ambani is one such personality. He was a poor person. Son of a schoolteacher. But had a strong willpower and capacity to put in hard work as well as business intellect. He had worked as a labor at a petrol pump for distributing the petrol. And later on, one day, he started distributing his own petrol pumps. How inspiring this story is. He raised his empire from a scratch.

The story of Kevin Care told by Poras Munshi is a similarly inspiring story. The specialty of G.K.

Ranganthan, the founder of Kevin Care, was that he estimated the market by himself roaming in the surroundings. Because of this, he came in direct contact with his customers and through this he could assess the mind of his customers first hand. He could assess the rise and fall in the market. Based on this, he made the necessary changes in his products and accordingly gave proper suggestions to his marketing team. Based on this, with just ₹ 15000/- in hand, he started his business. He did a turnover of ₹ 3 lakh in the first year. In the next year, his monthly turnover touched ₹ 4 lakh. Gradually, in 5-7 years this figure touched ₹ 750 crores. This one individual made this amazing achievement merely on the basis of his mental instinct. It cannot be said that he did not face obstacles. The hurdles were there; but he had the unique determination to overcome them. Based on this alone, he competed with giant companies like Hindustan Lever and Procter and Gamble. He found his own market and stamped his own identity.

That means, it is not a must that a big amount of capital is required to start any business. It is enough if you have a strong willpower. On the strength of this willpower, man can erase the word 'impossible' from his life. The word 'impossible' slows down a person's thought process. This word obstructs the intellect. Without the ghost of this word hovering on one's mind, a person begins to move his limbs with very minimum capital and raises an astounding business.

Walt Disney, the man who held the world spellbound, William Procter and James Gamble of Procter and Gambel who reigned over the world, commenced their life in such very difficult circumstances. But they started with a conviction and then never looked back. There is an interesting story about the first meeting between Procter and Gamble. They both were travelling in the same compartment of a train. Procter was busy reading a newspaper. By mistake, his feet touched that of the Gamble. Procter humbly said sorry to Gamble and thus started the first conversation and the relationship between the two big businessmen. Later on they married and their wives happen to be the sisters. They began their business from making of a soap and candle in a small way and now a leading multinational company, viz. P&G.

Just as, it is a myth that huge money is required to start business, so also people mistake destiny to have a great role in making a person, big in life. Frankly, 'destiny' is an imaginary thing. The main cause of your failure is your efforts falling short. Many people, instead of understanding this ground reality, like to keep harping on the failure. Opportunity knocks at every door not once, but several times. Finally to grab it and utilize it for our progress, is in our own hands. Along with this our inferiority complex judges our own capability. Therefore, many a time people hesitate to take new and different kind of decisions. Because of this the scope of each one of us too is a kind of state of the mind. If a person decides he can enhance his 'reach'.

Writer Shweta Ganu of Thane, in her book *Builder Vhaychay Mala* (*I Want to Become a Builder*) has given examples of all the three things. It is indeed exciting to read the stories of many renowned builders, without any background in the field and with not much financial backing, who entered the business, as portrayed by her in the book. But all of them have a common under-current.

When Mohan Deshmukh of Deshmukh Constructions, that has stamped its imprint in the construction sector, started his construction business, his father wrote him a letter. He instructed in the letter, "Remember one thing – Never do a fraudulent act for money."

Those words of Mohan Deshmukh's father are the guiding philosophy for many renowned builders, who have scaled heights of glory in the business sector. Integrity alone should be the basic foundation of any business.

If all the above three things are kept in mind then the foundation of any business will surely be strong. Without getting stressful about money, making efforts to raise the same, not giving much credence to destiny and without an inferiority complex utilizing your capabilities to the maximum extent are the *trimurti* (three-fold) elements of scripting success. It is a difficult path, but has hundred percent guarantee of success.

Money is a budding issue. It is true that without money in hand no one can start business. But those aspiring to start a new business, should have no reason to be frustrated and stop trying, if they actually do not have money in hand. It is true that money is required to start a business, but there is no rule that the money should be of the aspiring businessman. Do not forget that business should only be done on others' investment.

Today there are many legal means to raise money. There are several good schemes of the government to promote business. Now, without much complications, rules, and conditions, loans are given. But businessmen should study how to raise the money required by them. Without investing their own money, they should find means of raising money from other sources. Creditors will trust them only if their efforts appear fair. If the creditors feel that their enthusiasm is genuine, then they will lend without much hesitation. Only on the basis of their integrity and fairness, several big businessmen were given loans in the beginning stages of their business.

Start-up India is a very good initiative. All the banks will be coming forward to provide that most needed initial financial support to the budding businesses to start up. It is good to start with small. Your requirement, risk and also the rewards will be small. But must have that ambition to grow Big.

Success is sure if effort is put without losing courage. Two examples of veteran industrialist Neelkanth Kalyani are very striking. He had decided to give the work of preparing the project report of his company SIPCO to an American firm. However, the fees quoted were $45000 and that too in foreign currency. Kalyani went to Delhi to get this. He thought he would get the money in 2-3 days. In those days, he had to meet the Secretary in the Industry Department. But he could not meet him. The Secretary was always busy. Neelkanth Kalyani used to go to his office daily and wait for hours to meet him. During that very period his favorite uncle passed away. He became very concerned and confused. He could not leave the work half done.

Meanwhile the Secretary's brother-in-law expired. Therefore, he was in a hurry to rush to the airport. He saw Neelkanth Kalyani as he was coming out of his cabin. He realized that this young man has been waiting outside his office for many days. Neelkanth Kalyani met him and apprised him of his work. "We will meet after I return", the Secretary assured. That meant Kalyani had to wait for some more time. Kalyani too was at the airport to see the Secretary off. Coincidentally, the flight was cancelled. Therefore, he cancelled his going. Surprisingly, Kalyani brought him to his office in his car. "Now I have free time, what is your work?" he asked Kalyani. After hearing his request, he called his typist and dictated the order that was ready in 15 minutes. Neelkanth Kalyani was sanctioned the loan of $45000. His perseverance bore fruit.

There is one more similar incident. Kalyani always stuck to the discipline of not missing the date of giving salary to his employees. But once he did not have the money to pay on the salary day. The money did not come even on the last day of the month. It was a matter of his dignity to tell "I will not be able to give the salary as I do not have the money." He contacted the Chairman of Syndicate Bank, T.A. Pai. Mr. Pai called him to meet him in Mumbai. He heard him. Pai told him that he would come to visit his factory the next day. Surprisingly, Pai visited his factory the very next day. Seeing the work there, he became confident. He instructed the accompanying officials on the spot to grant him a loan of ₹ 20 lakh. Kalyani accomplished his work, due to his integrity, honesty, and passion.

Once a person is convinced of your honesty, he will go to any extent to co-operate with you. Once the loan seeker appears to be fair, then the obstructions are little. There may be problems in the very beginning. But once your determination is firm, and then they too can be surmounted. The example of Rajendra Bhagat, a businessman in Baramati is very telling. The owner of just

1.5 acres of land at home, he was gripped with the dream of trading. With very little money, he went to Singapore. He faced negative response at many places there. His money was getting over. Finally, utilizing all the money left with him, he summoned a press conference of representatives of traders. He explained his objective in broken English. The conference ended. He had only the money to buy a ticket to return home. With no response in two days, he returned home, to Pune, very disappointed. His dream of doing international trade was on the brink of being shattered. He could not think what to do. After two months in this condition, suddenly he got a mail from the representative of a Japanese trader. He wanted garlic. Rajendra received an order to supply 1000 kgs of garlic. Purchasing from nearby Baramati at ₹ 15-20 per kg, he sold them to Japan for ₹ 350-400 per kg. He earned much profit in this. Now, this youth trades with many countries in agricultural products. His turnover is in several crores today.

One incident of Rajendra is very amazing. He once got an order for lotuses from an American company. The best lotuses are grown in India. Rajendra decided not to back out from this order. He journeyed and selected lotuses near the Bhopal region. He plucked the closed lotus buds before sunrise. A chartered plane was kept ready. The plane reached America in 24 hours and next day at the decided time the company received the fresh Indian lotuses in full bloom. This is an example of the magic that a youth from an ordinary family can perform.

While setting up your business if you can be firm in your mind, then you too can do this magic. You alone are the only obstacle. If you take care of these emotional aspects that come in the way of progress, then you can easily find the path of progress. In this, the first challenge is your understanding of your capability. We set up limits, of our capability to do anything, in our mind. 'This is beyond my capacity,' or 'My limit ends here,' we announce this without hesitation. In this, many a time, it is your inferiority complex.

If we see in our individual life, the capacity of each person varies. The capacity of a scooter driver over that of a cyclist, and then in that order of a motor driver, a truck driver, an aeroplane pilot is much different and more than the earlier one. But at a closer look, there is not much difference in the people driving them. They are all men made up of the same material. The only difference is the challenge that they have accepted. It is also seen that bigger the challenge accepted by the person, bigger the capacity he has. Thus, we can conclude that "your capacity varies according to the challenges you accept". It needs to be understood that the capacity is not a physical parameter like weight, height, etc. of a person. It has limitation. Unlike this the capacity is a mental parameter. It has unlimited potential and depends on how much you can harness it. Therefore during strife or difficult times only, people do tasks many times over their known capacity. As per the same logic, the person cycling 10 kms daily can increase his capacity to cycle 15-20 kms daily. This only proves that capacity is, many a time, only a state of mind. This can be increased by willpower. That means, our capacity is always not the same forever. It is then, as the situation demands at a particular time. We should therefore understand the meaning of capacity.

Therefore, a person who has taken a step forward to start a new business should not under-estimate his own capacity. He should consistently try to increase his capacity with hard work. He should be mentally and physically prepared for challenges stretching his capacity. Meaning, everyone has capacity. We should prepare our mindset for that.

I asked a student, "what is the meaning of Luck? What are good luck, bad luck, and best luck? And does he believes in Luck at all?" He replied, "I do not know. Many people are not clear in their concept of luck, good luck, and bad luck." Yet they keep blaming it for failures. We hear the expression 'whatever is destined cannot be avoided,' time and again. Because of this attitude we do not believe in effort making. We avoid making effort. Nothing is achieved without effort.

A businessman too does not achieve anything through luck; he has to struggle for that. It is very essential to understand what is luck. I feel, 'where effort creases, luck commences.' After doing whatever is in our hands, after putting in all that you could, then there should be no objection to depend on luck for the rest of the work. There are many things beyond our control. We cannot say what will happen in those cases. Hence, we can attribute it to luck or destiny. Now let us understand what is the meaning of factors beyond your control. It simply means that those factors are in some body else's control. If that some body is helping me, then I can say I am lucky. But there are certain things, which are not in any body's control. May be its nature, etc. I think hereafter we can leave things to the destiny. So there are different zones for your efforts, your luck, and your destiny. This alone is the meaning of destiny. But there is no meaning to the naivety that "I will not do any thing and I will get whatever is in my destiny." It is wrong to surmise that, 'if there is my God, He will give me in bountiful.' God helps those who help themselves.

Everyone places a barometer of his destiny within himself (in his mind). He conjures an imaginary scale of 1 to 10 for his effort and then luck and then destiny will commence. But in the case of some people the scale for his effort is up to 20 or 30 and then the count of luck and destiny begins from 31. In the case of some, this limit can stretch to 50, 60, 80, 90, and 95. This means that if you decide you can decrease the quantum of luck and destiny. This power is known as willpower. If you have strong willpower, you will not be cowed down by any problems. Such people consider problems as opportunities. They never even utter the words 'destiny' or 'fate'. Everyone is aware of the story of Thomas Alva Edison. His laboratory was gutted in fire and all his instruments, equipment were burnt. But Edison was not disappointed. He said, "God is great. He has burnt all my mistakes. Now I can restart with new thesis and without mistakes." And within a month thereof, he invented a phonograph. No one can defeat a person with such an attitude. Veteran poet Harivanshrai Bachhan in one of his popular poems states, "Those who show courage never fail."

It is necessary to prepare a mindset to be so courageous before setting foot in the business sector. Renowned writer Shiv Khera has titled his book itself as *You can Win*. If it is so, then why fear?

"I find that the harder I work, the more luck I seem to have."

—Thomas Jafferson, Third President, USA

□

6

Obstacles in the Race

"Would you like me to give you a formula for success? It's quite simple, really; double your rate of failure. You're thinking of failure as enemy of success. But it isn't at all. You can be discouraged by failure, or you can learn from it. So go ahead and make mistakes. Make all you can. Because remember, that's where you will find success."

—**Thomas J. Watson,** ex-Chairman and CEO of IBM

Obstacles are bound to be there in whatever new venture you want to enter into. You should pledge yourself to the path of integrity if you have to surmount these obstacles. We can call this mentality as value system or ethics. We should adhere to this value system always in whatever we do. This adherence strengthens the foundation of our life. The tallest structures of our life can be built on this strong foundation. Lofty ideas such as integrity is in-built in this value system; but also simple issues like sticking to scheduled time, keeping one's word, fulfilling commitments are also incorporated in this value system. These things, that apparently look very simple, play a very big role in grooming your personality.

Increasing or reducing the value of your word (commitment) is in your own hands. The habit of simple things like sticking to the time promised reveals the person's viewpoint and in the long run this quality has very good effect. This becomes very useful in branding your personality and business.

You should think of success and failure in this context. In the course of business, many a time you become helpless at a certain turning point or to put it harshly you tend to become stupid in your reaction. You are unable to decide which turn to take at various turns that lure us on the path. This is the first obstacle on the race you are to run in life or business. The easiest and nearest turn lures you. The master key to overcome the first obstacle is to avoid the short cut and keep going. The firm trust on this path of integrity has made many businessmen renowned.

Ravindra Prabhaudeai, head of the Pitambari Group of Industries, has cited a memoir of his father. His grandfather had a grocery shop. But integrity was their family's forte. There was never a fraud about the goods in the shop. His father started a transport business. His faith and involvement in the business was so much that he used to lend a hand to the workers to reduce their burden. He once wanted a loan. Banks asked for a surety. He had nothing to hypothecate. He collected the receipts of all the installments paid of the previous loans and presented it to the bank. The regularly paid installments were proof of his integrity and fairness. The bank officials considered these valid and gave him the loan without any security. Prabhudesai attributes the whole success of the Pitambari Group to this integrity brand of the family. Merely on the basis of this branding, his Pitambari product reaches 50 lakh customers through over 1000 distributors in 16 States in the country and in many other countries in the world.

You can easily overcome the problem of capital if you have integrity and fairness. The first issue that comes to mind to start any business is capital. The simple meaning is that from where to bring money to start a business. Here I have to make one point clear, it will be crazy to assume that to start a business one has to be as big as Tata, Birla or Ambani, or it has to start only in that large proportion. These business empires were not established overnight. All the big business groups started generally from modest beginnings. At the very outset, you must discard the thought from your mind that I will start only when I have enough money to start big or else I will not start, in the spirit as a regional saying goes, "I will eat only with ghee or else starve." But at the same time must also bear in mind that some money will be required to start any business. Business without capital in a way is a poetic imagination. Many a time, this capital is not in the form of money but in the form of intellectual skill or capability. Even though it is said that business should always be done with others' money, then also people will invest only if they see profitability in the business.

When you think of whose money it could be, then three segments come to mind: (i) Banks, (ii) Investors, and (iii) Customers. This has been told earlier, but here I will present the same in slightly different manner. The network of banks has spread today on a large scale all over the nation and into traders, urban centers, co-operatives, and agricultural sectors. Earlier the banks did not have such a large network. Therefore, there was little scope to get bank loans. Today due to various government policies, it has become much easier to get loan from banks. Today banks have huge money. They have to lend to customers to increase their business. Only a certain amount of trust-worthiness is required. Banks have several schemes. You have to fit your business-profession into those schemes. You have to bear one thing in mind here; all your documents should be lawful and legal and you should follow all rules and regulations fully. No one can stop you from getting a loan if you are lawful in all aspects.

The other segment that provides funds for business is the investors. Today there are many people loaded with money. These people are not satisfied with the rate of interest given by banks. They want to earn a little more than that. But they do not intend to do any business of their own or are not capable of doing hard work taking care of the various hurdles. They only are ready to invest in some business that has profitability and credibility. If you can instill trust in the mind of such investors, you can easily get money from them. In the beginning, you can raise such funds from your friends and relatives. There is no problem in considering such people as your investors, when you are going to sincerely return their money with interest.

The third option to raise capital is directly from the customers. In transactions, this is called as advance or taking money in advance. A simple example of this, in our daily dealing is many businesses run by the women 'self help groups'. People doing such business take advance money from the customers in the beginning itself. With that they buy the required raw materials and manufacture products, which are sold to the customers. Their business runs on the profits earned from this. Such booking amounts can be taken for any business. Such advances are generally taken/given for vehicles, homes and even for books. Previously, the booking period for Bajaj scooters used to be 8-10 years in advance. Since the Bajaj brand was astonishingly very popular, customers too would happily book and wait eagerly for the scooter. Bajaj scooters were a status symbol then. Advance booking is also done for books by renowned authors. In tourism business too, advance is taken for booking tours. One basic thing for this is that the customers should have hundred percent faith in the quality of your product and your fairness. You can also announce some attractive discounts/concessions to attract customers who pay in advance. Rather businessmen compete to give such concessions/discounts to attract more and more customers. Pre-launch offers in projects too fall in this category.

Considering all the above three options, sometimes businessmen prefer to start business with their own money than to raise money in the above ways. But the business of those, who think so, cannot last for long nor rise to big heights. The main reason being that there is limit to people's individual wealth. Besides, such money has to be kept in reserve with oneself as contingency fund for difficult times in business. Therefore, it is necessary to raise money from all possible sources and utilize it in business. This is called leveraging.

Lord Shri Krishna had taken the assistance of every individual possible when he lifted the Govardhan mountain. Looking at the incredible power of Shri Krishna, it was not impossible for him to do this on his own. But he wanted everybody's participation in that. Hence, it is necessary to raise money from all possible sources for business. Shri Krishna only touched the mountain with his little finger. The young and old of Gokul lent their strength to lift the mountain and achieve the great task. We have to underline the most important point in this. That is, all the young, old, and the poor people had firm faith that Shri Krishna would protect them from the catastrophic rain. If businessmen earn such unquestionable credibility, then there will be no hurdle at all to raise capital with the help of banks, investors, and customers.

Even after crossing the first hurdle for capital, businessmen have apprehensions in their mind about the success or failure. Even though money has been raised from various efforts, a common man flinches while actually starting business. He is always tense in his mind with the calculation of profit-loss. One thing is clear; nobody can make profit without taking risk. The main thought in anybody's mind, while starting business, is that of profit. He links this calculation of profit to his success and failure. In fact, business is a journey and not a destination. It is a process. Likewise success and failure both are journeys and not the destinations. They are not the ends. They are the part and parcel of life.

John C. Maxwell narrates a very good principle about this in his book titled *Failing Forward*. In public life, a person has to confront success and failure at sometime or the other. It is an unavoidable part of life. Because of this failure or success, one's mind is affected by despair or arrogance respectively. Generally, "success goes to the head, which may develop arrogance and failure goes to the heart, causing him to sink in despair" and if the severity is more may cause heart failure. This means that success affects a person's head that is his thinking and failure affects his heart that is his feelings. What should actually happen is the reverse of this. That is the success should go to the heart which will make you humble and the failure should go to the head where it will be analysed. Your intellect should take note of your failure, which means, that when you fail, you should think about it seriously, as to why you failed. Accordingly, you should change your working method. On the other hand, you should become more magnanimous due to your success. You should realize that this success is not due to your effort alone, but the fruit of a collective effort. Acknowledging that you alone do not have the right to the joy of this success, you should distribute this joy to everyone. Success should be balanced in the heart. The head should give deep thought and analyse the failure, without wounding the heart. Thus, even the heart will not be adversely affected.

There is one more angle to this story of success and failure. That says, there is no success without a failure. In fact, failure is treated as stepping stone for the success. That means if you want to succeed, you must fail. And it is also said that bigger the failure bigger will be the success.

If you are conscious of success and failure concept, then your struggle assumes a moral platform and your effort finds a human face. Renowned industrialist Kalpana Saroj's example is an inspiration for all time. Kalpana Saroj, from earning a daily wage of ₹ 2/- during her days of struggle, went on to achieve a turnover of ₹ 2000 crore. She went to Mumbai to find a way, having married at the age of only 12 undergoing much torture in her in-law's place and poverty condition of her father, who was a havaldar. She somehow got shelter at a Gujarati's house, somehow managed a job at a stitching workshop on a daily wage of ₹ 2/- and learnt stitching work. She purchased a machine by doing extra work. Work kept increasing. She combined her mental determination with her readiness to work hard. Kalpana Saroj is now the chairperson of Kamani Tubes, a company with a turnover in the range of ₹ 2000/- crore. In my view, success can be defined in one word. That word is 'hard work.' Kaplana Saroj states "If you work hard then success is certain." But what she states further is very important: "In whatever you do, your objective should be very clear, pure, and transparent. If people do not suspect your intention then half the battle is won," she insistently asserts.

After moving ahead from the first stage of raising capital, without worrying about success and failure and continuously working hard, means, laying the foundation of your business. When you succeed in this, digest it in a balanced way and with a magnanimous mind include many people in it. In failure, think about it with a peaceful mind, carve a path out of this. Any business is a long-term race of obstacles and further in this, the actual commencement of business stage is as important as this.

A man must be big enough to admit his mistakes, smart enough to profit from them, and strong enough to correct them.

—**John C. Maxwell,** CEO of The John Maxwell Company

□

7

Planning and Implementation

"The best way to get started is to quit talking and begin doing."

—**Walt Disney,** famous as a pioneer of cartoon films and as the creator of Disneyland

After raising capital, it is imperative to immediately start implementation, as per the planning in your mind. At this time you have to take some decision on the shape of your business and your objective. Among the various inspirations to do business/profession, the most important inspiration is the monetary profit. The quantum of profit in the business is a very sensitive issue. The proportion of profit in any business/profession is decided on different factors. The proportion of profit depends on, the kind of raw materials you use, the cost of raw materials, the cost of transportation of the raw material to the factory, the cost of transportation of the finished product to the market and the cost of employees' salary. Taking into consideration all these, a businessman should decide the profit he wants.

It is okay if turnover is reduced. But many businessmen initially feel that they should get huge profit. The reason behind that is to recover their invested money instantly. But there is a possibility of being cheated in this, many a time. There is no short cut to earn profit in any business. The suddenly increased profit spells doom at the same speed. Today, there is stiff competition in every field. Hence, several alternatives to your product keep entering the market at a fast pace. Hence, you have to draw a proportion of your business and profit to stay firm in the market for a long time in such a situation. Today there are actually thousands of products in the market. Yet why do only the following names come to mind like 'Jai Kajal' for kajal, 'Nag brand Hing' for hing, 'Dalda' for vanaspati ghee and 'Godrej' for locks and cupboards, Sony-iPhone-Samsung? Because there is a passionate perseverance, for a long time, behind these products. A permanent bond has been created between these products and their customers. It is more important, to create such a relationship for your product, to increase your turnover, instead of more profits and to reach your product to more people. Today, customers are attracted to the reach of any product. If 'Rasna' goes to every home, then 'Rasna' becomes a status symbol. Several detergent powders entered the market but none could match the reach of 'Nirma'. The manufacture of Nirma may not have kept a large margin on the printed price on the pack, but he targeted a larger customer base and every home. Hence, even after advertising by three generations of girls, the popularity of 'Nirma' continues to last. This manufacturer has implemented the best formula of success – 'less profit and more turnover.'

If the customer-base widens, then the cost of overheads of the product reduces and profits increase without raising costs. Therefore, efforts should be made to reach your product to the maximum customers, rather than earning more profits. You will realize that more the customers, more the satisfaction and thereby more the profits. This increasing number of customers alone will give you more profits. Therefore, it is necessary to keep in mind that 'Customer is Business', 'Customer is Profit.' Take care of your customers, business will be automatically taken care of, every businessman should bear this in mind.

Before planning and implementation, you cannot move forward without deciding the nature of your business and what business you exactly intend to do. There are thousands of choices actually about choosing a business. It can be said that sky is the limit in this. That means this choice will have to be made depending upon your capacity, skill, and capital. At the same time, you have to calculate in your mind the usefulness of your product. If you have the passion to do something then there is no dearth of products to be manufactured by a resourceful businessman.

The example of Suresh Muley of Chirantan Service in Thane, a city of Maharashtra is astonishing. A qualified engineer Suresh Muley was mentally inclined to writing. He has several dramas, clear essays, and humorous writings to his credit. He had casually read news of Pimpri-Chinchwad Municipal Corporation wanting to import an electric crematorium. Suresh Muley became very restless reading that even a thing like electrical crematorium has to be imported. He told his corporate friend, Dinkar Damle of Thane Municipal Corporation that "there is nothing in an electric crematorium that we have to import them. We can easily make it in our country." Damle was convinced of his idea and with the joint efforts of both, 'Chirantan Services' was born. This company's product was electrical crematorium. Chirantan Services manufactured 35 electrical crematoriums in a 10 years span from 1998 to 2008. The cost of one electric crematorium is around ₹ 40 lakh. In this business, Suresh Muley did neither erect a factory nor recruit employees. He gets the electric crematorium manufactured in others' factory as per the design required by the municipality. He, however, did the maintenance with his personal attention. It is true that it cannot be said from where the 'Business' will arrive.

That means, the manufacturer should seriously think about the utility of his product along with his resourcefulness. 'Pitambari' industry is an ideal in this respect. This business was born out of the resourcefulness of Ravindra Prabhudesai. He was gripped by the passion to do his own business. Being associated with the Rashtriya Swayamsevak Sangh, he had a huge network of contacts. He had gone to the homes of many people, in the course of his work with the Sangh. Seeing the copper vessels and brass boxes in many homes, his mind started breeding the urge to do something to keep these vessels shining clean. From this was born 'Pitambari' powder. In the beginning, it was publicized by distributing free samples. Ravindra Prabhudesai was basically very resourceful. He first gave free samples to the Taj Hotel directly. The management there liked it so much that they immediately placed an order for 50 kg. This was his company's first big order. After that there was no looking back for 'Pitambari'. Today it has reached almost every state in the country and also crossed national borders.

Started in a small house in the state, 'Pitambari' is today manufactured in factories in many cities.

This indicates the necessity of manufacturing products that are of daily use to the people. The principle that selecting the right product is half the battle won, wholly applies in this case.

The above two examples have been intentionally cited while referring to the planning and implementation of business. You can discover business in anything and if the product is of daily use to the people then there will be no dearth of sales; this is evident from the above example.

Along with the above two things, your mind should have an eternal obsession for innovation. Only with this obsession can you be useful for innovative research. Therefore, it will be wrong to surmise in business that once you start a business you resolve not to change anything. Though, initially, the business will be started, yet without change and progress it will collapse soon.

A massive showcase containing each and every product manufactured by the globally renowned Japanese company 'Sony' has been decoratively displayed at the company's corporate office in Tokyo. The model of every product manufactured by Sony till date is displayed there. In the starting line the first product displayed is a 'cooker', yes indeed 'a cooker.' Sony Company started with the very manufacture of a cooker. Today Sony manufactures the most ultra-modern products, that we cannot think of relating Sony to pressure cookers. So every business should have obsession for improvement and innovation.

Anyone can do his own business on the capital of mental instinct, choice of product and a constant preparedness for research and innovation. It is enough to have little capital and the readiness to work hard. At the root of all this is the significant 'self-confidence.' You should have faith about your self in your mind in whatever you undertake to do. Without this you can do nothing. One cannot give a cent percent guarantee about being successful always, when you start a new business. But you should be mentally prepared to digest success and failure. Without being bogged down by failure, you should overcome it and find new ways through it. This can happen only when you are firmly self-confident.

Success and failures can be phases of the journey. They cannot be the final destinations. Failure is the first step in the direction of success. We should understand the relationship between them. It is true that nobody gets success instantly, but it is not true that the road to success goes through failure only. Success is a thing that does not depend on destiny alone. Thus, it can be achieved with efforts. Hence, everyone should accept success with humility. This means success should permeate his heart. He should include everybody in it. On the other side, without despairing about failure, he should analyze his failure. He should diagnose his failure with a cool head. He can learn much from this failure and his path to success will become easy.

Success depends on one more thing. That is your decision-making power. Only people who have flawless decision-making power can take instant decisions at the right time. Loss is certain in any field even if one wrong decision is made. In business, the loss, due to wrong decisions, is many times more. There is a constant threat of the whole business sinking due to one faulty decision.

In the construction business, which is capital intensive, the risk of this happening is very high. The importance of timing in cricket, politics or dialogue delivery in drama, is the same of decision making in business. It is not merely a part of co-incidence that capacity to take decisions is related to intelligence. Study, penance, and concentration are required for this capacity. Many people have the habit of keeping important decisions pending. Such people can never get spectacular success. Decisions must be made fast and if any decision goes wrong, it should be corrected too, fast. Holes should be filled when they are tiny. 'Stitch in time saves nine' is a very apt saying for business.

V.G. Siddharth of Chikmangalur had coffee plantations. Coffee is made from the seeds of coffee trees grown in farms. Whatever be the price of ready coffee in the market, the coffee harvested by the farmer gets paid very less. Siddharth has several plantations of coffee, but he was too trapped in this vicious cycle. But an idea struck his mind at a moment. He strongly realized that instead of selling coffee seeds, if he sells well-made, hot coffee, this will certainly attract the youngsters. The concept of Café Coffee Day was born out of this. His market was the youthful boys and girls. These boys and girls wanted a place where they would not be asked to leave, irrespective of the time they sit. Café Coffee Day became a place of right for these youngsters who could converse to their heart's content with their boy and girl friends or view their Facebook on laptop or e-mails while enjoying their drink of coffee. Those centers become very popular, with customers thronging in large numbers. These centers were vibrant with the enthusiasm of the youngsters. Soon the Café Coffee Day stalls sprung up in many cities. It crossed a hundred cities before long. This is the best example of how a business flourishes if supported by resourcefulness.

The planning and implementation of a business depends upon the thinking of the businessman. If your thought is firm, then erecting the said business is not difficult. Any business is a sapling initially. This sapling has to be nurtured with the water of the businessman's effort and the manure of his honesty. It has to be protected from heat and wind. If it becomes impossible with singular effort then the support of several loyalists has to be gathered. The relation of the businessman with every section of the community becomes significant to garner such assistance.

"Success is not final, Failure is not fatal; It is the courage to continue that counts."

—**Winston S. Churchill,** Prime Minister of UK (1945-55)

□

8
Relations

"It takes 20 years to build a reputation and five minutes to ruin it. If you think about that, you'll do things differently."

—**Warren Buffett,** CEO of Berkshire Hathaway

Business is not what one person has to do. It is a collective, team process. It is a teamwork. Therefore, where more than one person come together, their mutual relations, have to be thought about. The definition of any collective process is the establishment of relations with many people and encouraging everyone towards the direction of one objective. These relations have a decisive significance in any business.

The affection for every employee was a special feature of the Kirloskar Group of Industries. Veteran industrialist Late Shantanurao Kirloskar had set this ideal. He considered the workers, employees of the Kirloskar Group as his family. Once rice had become very costly during his reign. It came to Kirloskar's notice that the cost of rice had increased a great deal. He was saddened by the thought of how expensive it must be for his workers to buy rice. A thought came to his mind that if he purchased rice from the wholesale market, he could give it to his workers at cheaper price. He immediately discussed it with his officials. The scheme was implemented. Workers of the Kirloskar Group started getting rice at a lesser cost. Relations are built on small, small issues. S.R. Patil the president of Datta Cooperative Sugar Mill sits on a very ordinary wooden chair. His chair is just like that of a clerk's or a teacher's. Due to the simplicity realized through this chair, he could intimately connect instantly with the person in front of him.

Veteran industrialist and the chief of the Tata Group of Industries Ratan Tata had such friendly relation with his workers. Prior to his retirement, he had come to the Telco Company in Pune. After the farewell function, a collective luncheon was organized. Ratan Tata savored his meal in the common canteen of the workers, sitting in line with the workers. He openly participated in their fun and frolic.

The wives of the workers are free throughout the day. The directors of Telco felt that if their work force was utilized, they could be given employment sitting at home. Renowned to be a strict disciplinarian, Shri Mehrunkar was the Managing Director of Telco then. He was strict, but his affection for the workers was overwhelming. He implemented the idea and started a big business for the women of the workers family of household products like pickles and papad.

'Shramik' the housing project built by Haware Builders, fructified out of this unique pull of 'Relations.' This was a dream project of Satish Haware. Even a common man dreams of owning his own home. This project fulfilled that dream. This Shramik project negated the understanding that the idea of owning one's own home involves a cost running into lakhs or crores of rupees. 200 poor people like handcart pullers, fruit-vegetable sellers, rickshaw drivers, vada-pav vendors, tea sellers, got houses in this project at a minimum cost. The dream of the own house of these common people could be possible due to the 'relations' maintained by Satish Haware, the revered construction professional. He is no more today. But residents of Shramik project have placed his photo in their place of worship at home.

Then such is the 'relations'-sensitive businessmen maintain. Where more than one person come into contact, there this 'relations' assume very great significance. A business stands only if this relation is maintained. Any business thrives only on this relation. The chain built by these relations is known as network. In a nation that has a big chain of businesses, this network is automatically set in place.

Shri Madhavrao Bhide established the Saturday Club to increase relations among businessmen and help them grow their business through networking. The club has thousands of branches in India and abroad. Madhavrao Bhide is an 86 years old young man bubbling with enormous energy. A meeting with him is very inspirational. He has kept his club's mission as – 'Let us assist each other and make everyone rich.'

Just as there is this relation between the employer and worker, so also it is mutually built among workmen. So also it exists between businessmen and the customers. Those who want success in their profession have to maintain this good relation. In the community that has a great tradition of business, the character of maintaining relations among their people is inbred. This kind of networking takes shape easily in such a community. Those who do not have such inborn tradition, they can build it with effort.

The network of such relations is very useful in the growth of business. But these relations or network is not built in a day. Nor is it built merely by talking or knowing each other. But it is built on the constant transactions of faith. Transaction can take place once an acquaintance is established. Once faith is experienced in a transaction, then this can happen many times. The network of relations is built ultimately out of the good relation established with one person and then with many in the same manner. Once this network is built, then it becomes very easy to set up a new business model, as investors are waiting to participate with confidence. This network is very important in the business of those whose businesses are established and growing.

It is important to understand people. Any business is finally a transaction between people. Those who want to properly establish their profession; they will have to take good care of their transaction with people. For this, an individual intending to set up a business, should first imbibe the art of reading or recognizing people. Many people have this inbred art. Shivaji Maharaj should be considered an ideal for this capability. It is difficult to find another leader with as much capacity to read a person in front of him. Therefore, every person to whom Shivaji Maharaj handed over the work, was all successful. Shivaji Maharaj got exemplary work done by people who looked very ordinary and less capable. Maharaj could do this because of his capacity to assess people's merit.

Businessmen too should be able to judge people around him in his pursuit of success. The other meaning of this is that he should be able to read people. He should have an x-ray vision of the experiences that comes his way every moment. Penetrating through the people's eyes, he should be able to grasp what is in their mind. There is money in business and hence many needy, wanting, unwanted elements gather around for money. He should be able to dissect, after a little acquaintance, the selfless and loyal among them, who are hard working and who are greedy. He should screen away the selfish and unreliable people while building a network of trustworthy people. The vision of the businessman should be penetrating to be able to read the mind of the person in front of him, but at the same time it should be comforting to instill hope to the people in front of him.

Since business is ultimately related to marketing and trade, the development of business is through meeting and contacts. A businessman should be able to judge within two minutes what work the man in front of him, has. The businessman should take care that the customer should not go back disappointed. Even if the customer does not get the product he wants, it is okay; but he should not be disappointed. The businessman should ensure this. It can be done with the businessman's simple talk. If you win the confidence of the customer, then he will come back to you the next time. The special thing about this is that the businessman has to do all this only with his talk. Giving relief and hope with your talk and attaching him to you forever is what is called as 'relations!' 'Customer is God' should be the basic principle of any business and under any circumstance the customer should be taken good care of. The principle should be 'never allow customers to break away.'

Yallasha Gigmal Kamble who grew up at Sewri's labor camp was somehow managing the affairs of his family with his small business. Looking at the increased price of real estate in Mumbai, the thought of owning his own house was an impossible dream from his point of view. Yet he once visited a property exhibition. There were all kinds of big and small projects in many, varied decorative stalls. The stalls were attractive and luring. But the price of the house in his scheme of things, from a common man's point of view, was impossible to get. "I cannot afford these houses, rather the idea of a house does not fit into the mathematics of my revenue", this thought germinated in his mind. He began feeling that the attractive stalls there were now teasing him. As he was coming out with a disheartened mind, his attention was drawn towards the stall of Haware Constructions. The mission statement there – "people who realize your dream of a home", gave him a big assurance. The advertisement there – 'Pay ₹ 5000/- and book your home of ₹ 2.5 lakh' drew his attention. Kamble understood the scheme. He liked the scheme very much. A new hope blossomed in his disheartened mind. He wanted to instantly book a house. But as he had casually come to the exhibition, he did not have that much money. The executive in the stall told him, "If you do not have ₹ 5000/- now pay a little less. But book a house." Kamble was feeling hesitant to tell him. He had just ₹ 100/- with him. The representative in the stall told him, "you can pay just ₹ 100/- only and register your name." "It was the promoter of the project, Satish Haware's instruction that the 'Shramik' project was for the working class and hence even if they have less money do not deny them. They should never feel that they lost the opportunity to book a house due to, not having money in their pockets," the representative told him thus and he felt, he had met a messenger of God. Booking a house, he went home overjoyed.

Not Kamble alone, but among the home buyers in this scheme there are 200 people's stories like that of Panditrao Salunkhe, a mill worker, Umesh Nadgam, drawing a monthly salary of ₹ 2500/-, Sadanand Bhilare, an autorickshaw driver in Vashi and Anand Kamble, resident of a small room in a chawl in Chembur a suburb of Mumbai. This project was realized from the faith in the concept of maintaining 'relations.' Be it customers or employees of your business group, businessmen should maintain an emotional bond with them. Through this alone they will be linked to your business permanently. Taking care of relations is the basic foundation of marketing. Rather, good relations by a different name is called marketing. Where the base is love and integrity, such marketing becomes hundred percent successful and this success lasts long. The secret of success of many businesses, lasting through generations braving difficulties, heat and storm, is this.

Your language and your body language are both very important while taking care of these relations. From this alone your exclusiveness is imprinted in the customers' mind. Their exclusiveness is not merely what shows on the surface, it is not cosmetic. But it has gone deep touching the very root of your company's policy. Japanese companies have competed with mighty American companies and left their mark on world trade on the strength of their qualities of work capability, fairness, and persuasive talk. Japan was literally reduced to ashes in the Second World War. The two atom bombs that America dropped on the two cities Nagasaki and Hiroshima had literally broken the back of Japan but Japan took flight like the Phoenix bird from this total devastation. This flight literally stunned the whole world. The credit for this revolution by Japanese businessmen should go to the workers and the market as also to the special kind of relations maintained by the Japanese business groups. Japanese companies are very particular in the selection of workers. In Japan, once a worker accepts a job in a company, he normally does not leave the job and the company too does not easily leave that person. These companies normally recruit employees through campus interviews. They put in everything to teach the employee everything. They train the employee in every department of the company. They give him the work experience. The employee's promotion depends on his work experience. The companies take full care of such employees. Hence, the company establishes a permanent bond with the employees. This brings profit to the company and there is stability in the life of the employees. Due to such employees alone, 'Sony' company of Japan established its supremacy all over the world.

Public contact is also included in the kind of relations. However, good a particular product of a company may be, yet public relation is needed to imprint it in people's mind and to build a brand image. In the initial stages, when the company is small, the owner plays the various roles of the management, say marketing, advertising, and distribution. At that time he has to take care of the public relation department too. But as the scale of work of the company increases so also the need of an independent public relation department arises. Then the need arises to appoint a public relation officer. This officer reaches the good points of the company to the public and a specific customer base. He tries to build a good image of the company among the mass of people. He addresses the issues of the customers and the vendors and replies to doubts and suspicions. He also gives a feedback of the opinion about the product of the company in the market and among the customers, to the officials. In a way the public relations officer tries to preserve the relations between the company and the customers. In a way every employee of the company is the public relations officer of that company. Leaving aside working hours of the employee, people look at him as a representative of the company only. Just as every Indian abroad is considered in a way to be the country's ambassador, so also it is about the employees. Hence, the behavior and body language of these employees are very important.

Even from the ordinary talk of any person, his culture and his thinking can be gauged. Hence, every word uttered by any employee of a company among the general public creates a good or bad opinion about the company. The role of these employees becomes very significant in preserving the relations of the company. The tone of a conversation changes when you say, "What you say may be right, but what I am saying too is right," instead of, "What I am saying alone is right." From the viewpoint of the profitability of a company, to be able to catch that tone, good conversation is important and building relations and preserving the relations is very important. Due to this role the name of the government's labor department is named as Shram (effort/hard work) Mantralaya. In various companies now the personnel department for employees is known as Human Resource Development department. Maintaining the morale of the employees constantly is essential for the progress of the company. This morale is sustained by the relations with the employee and the customer.

'People is Business' is a term often used in the business sector. Similarly, it is also said, 'Relation is Business'. Ultimately, any business is for the society that is for the people only. This person may be an associate, employee, investor or customer or anybody else. All these comprise a team. Even if one member of the team is pained, then everyone in the team is affected. From this, the conflict goes on increasing and then it does not take time for the whole business to sink to the deepest pit. But this sinking team can also sail the business to prosperity. Therefore, taking care of people should be the main objective of any business.

Business, profession or services are all related to money. But it is a misunderstanding that people are retained, due to money or people leave a job, for money. People need love, sense of belonging, and respect. Even if one customer is hurt, then he can create an island of poison against you. One hurt customer can influence ten other customers against you. On the contrary, one satisfied customer can provoke other ten customers to come to you. That means by satisfying one hurt customer and converting him into a happy customer, you can get ten new customers. Hence, instead of putting a board in bad taste like 'Cash today, Credit tomorrow,' putting 'Customers' Satisfaction is our Profit' could resolve the issue much more easily.

If you want to walk fast, walk alone. But if you want to walk far, walk together.

—**Ratan Tata,** ex-Chairman of Tata Sons

□

9

Branding

"We presume that it is okay if a project does not take off than to give bribe or stoop. And only because of this, the name 'Tata' will last."

—J.R.D. Tata

If you want a mobile, it must be of Samsung! or iPhone. You want a T.V.? There is no alternative to Sony. Pen? Only Parker! In the much earlier days just as Prabhakar lanterns and Ogale glass had invaded every home. In those times, in every home clothes used to be washed with 'Sunlight' soap and every house had a 'Godrej' Cupboard.

The product, be it big or small – they became brands in the mind of the customers. Customers get disappointed if they do not get the branded product of their choice. They cannot accept any other product. They are prepared to move around to search for their choice brands.

The emotion stirred by a product in the mind of the customers is what is known as the brand of that company. This brand is actually the company's name, logo, or initials. Even though these things are related to the product on view, the brand is close to the feeling about the company or about the product. For, an emotional bond is set between the customer and that product. Bedekar gives an experience of this in the advertisement for his world famous pickles. Bedekar has himself done this advertisement. In that he has said, only two people make good pickles. One is you and when you do not have the time then we. This single advertisement built incredible affection for Bedekar pickles all over. It is true that Bedekar pickles became a brand due to the taste of the pickles he maintained, attractive packing, and easy availability. But the foundation of the brand was laid by that emotional appeal. Once the emotional structure is set, then the brand of the product is ready by itself. This brand last for years and years in your mind and in the market forever.

Have you ever thought that 'Vicks', 'Amrutanjan' or 'Cherry Blossom' have been parked in your mind and homes for generations? Even to buy an ordinary bulb, then why do we instantly ask for 'Philips'? We do so, because, this product is distinct from the other kinds of the same product in the market. This product has preserved its distinctiveness year after year and they have stamped it in your mind ever since you have been able to understand things. The struggle to bring out this distinctiveness in your product and how to make it last for years and years is what is known as business. For this alone, taking care of all other troubles and work, business is run.

This is certainly asked about by any investor when you start a business and by the customer after the business commences. Because, the success of any business is hidden in this very distinctiveness. If you are not able to spell out this distinctiveness, then it becomes difficult to get a loan easily. And once the business starts and you fail to maintain this distinctiveness, then it will be difficult to retain your customers. This alone in business parlance is known as your business brand. Once this brand registers in the mind of the investors initially and then of the customers, then there is no looking back for the business.

However, if you are unable to convince them about your distinctiveness, then these people will turn to your competitors. They never go alone. They divert even those who intend to come to you. Hence, every businessman should strive, from the very beginning, to build their brand, keeping their distinctiveness intact.

This brand is not built by waving a magic wand. For this years and years of research, focus, perseverance, performance, integrity, and public relation are very much needed. Of this the most important thing is trust. Whether you deal in gold-silver or sand, this trust is your main capital and your brand is built, based on this trust. For years, people have been buying gold from P.N. Gadgil or Waman Hari Pethe, because of their blind trust in them that they will not cheat a paisa out of anyone. You are aware of the 'Anchor' brand, the manufacturer of electrical goods, when the company was shut, then that alone has been sold for over ₹ 400 crore. These filmy-like situations are no co-incidences. For this you have to prepare a chain of abilities and trust.

The story of Bhausaheb Kulkarni of 'Aashida', makers of extra high-voltage and easier automation products, is the story of how one individual, starting from one small room a business of home industries became a big brand – an amazing but equally touching saga.

Manohar alias Bhau Kulkarni started Aashida Company in 1970. He had just one worker then. He started his work in a 10×12 ft. room. His first year's turnover was just ₹ 1 lakh. Having crossed ₹ 50 crore turnover recently, the company is heading towards a ₹ 100 crore turnover. To reach this stage, if you see the focus and hard work of the Aashida team, you will realize that building a brand is indeed a penance. The result of this penance is that Aashida products are now sold in Philippines, Saudi Arabia, Germany, China and other countries.

Bhau sculpted Aashida in a special mould. Only because of this Aashida got its own identity. The statue of Mother India (Bharat Mata) in Aashida's office, the idol of Lord Ganesha near the entrance and the Sanskrit verse on the walls give a glimpse of the cultural identity of the company, but it also ratifies that lifeline of this business is linked to the life of people in this country. Bhau has outlined a statement of discipline and culture for the employees of Aashida. This is based on, "we will keep our quality even above the expectation of our customers." In this the maximum importance has been given to the company's moral stand and there is an unwritten law that the company will never misuse and cheat its customers, employees, suppliers, government, society, and Nature. The company insists on every employee keeping in mind every moment the fact that they should not consider the business as a means of livelihood, but a very great social responsibility. The company stresses on every employee behaving responsibly and not cheating any one anytime. Hence, the company should strictly adhere to this morality even at the cost of bearing losses, should the occasion arise, urges Bhausaheb and on this standing alone he has erected the company.

Now this morality or the moral standing or the evidence of integrity is what can be termed as the company's branding. Indian people were, so to say, backward in the field of tourism. It would have been difficult to believe, fifty years ago if anyone had said that it would a very high income-generating sector. Today tourism is a front ranking business. By using their ingenuity, the Gujarat Government appointed veteran cine star Amitabh Bachhan as their State ambassador for tourism, and catapulted Gujarat to the number one state in the country in tourism. Companies like 'Kesari Tours and Travels' of Maharashtra have taken big strides in this profession; but now this profession is not limited to taking domestic tourists to foreign countries alone, but is taking on new challenges of bringing foreign tourists to India. Kesaribhau Patil, the founder director of Kesari Tours has himself built this brand. The spread of Kesari Tours was not made possible overnight. The story behind it is amazing. Kesaribhau left his earlier family business due to a domestic dispute without a penny in his hand. The only thing he had was an unflinching resolve of the mind and willpower to scale heights. A teacher by profession, Kesaribhau's priority in business was fairness and integrity. Also, being an experimental farmer basically, the passion to perform new experiments was in his blood. These two qualities were extremely beneficial to him in this profession.

Kesaribhau started 'Kesari Travels' in a 10×10 sq.ft space in Dalmia Chawl on Kataria road in Mahim (Mumbai) in 1984. There were only 13 tourists in the first tour that he organized. Any tour organizer would have cancelled taking such a small group on tour. But Kesaribhau felt "If I back out now, then I will never be able to start." Those who did not have faith in our company did not turn up. But what right do I have to betray, in a way, or disappoint those who trusted us, he felt. He properly completed the tour. Since then his organization never looked back. Many people with vested interests tried very hard to put obstacles in his way. They advertised against him. But Kesaribhau decided that instead of fighting with them, he would give a fitting reply with his work. Tourists liked the distinctiveness in his company's tours. The number of tourists in his tours grew. Today 'Kesari' has become the leading tour organizer in the country. Today, during the tours season, Kesari organizes 80 to 90 tours at a time. He has proved the company's slogan – 'Trusted name in conducted tours.' He has realized the statement 'spreading smiles and happiness' on the strength of quality service and trust-worthiness. 'Kesari' should be considered an ideal example of how a 'brand' is born through the determination to brave harsh odds and willpower.

Veena Patil, who had to exit from 'Kesari' family business, due to unavoidable circumstances, started a new business Veena World in a very short span of three months time. She started organizing tours and in a short time established her brand. Everybody felt that this company was as experienced and old as Kesari Tours. While giving an interview to IBN Lokmat, Veena Patil's eyes were moist with tears as she was talking about the domestic affairs. But if she had become disappointed and frustrated, our country would have lost a new business. But she easily digested her sorrow and pain and stood up. This is special about her. I have always been saying that we must be able to convert our adversity into opportunity. Veena has proved this. Family dispute is not an incomprehensible event. Expecting it after a certain period, it will be good to re-structure the business on your own. But one thing came good out of this. Instead of one option for going on tours, now tourists had two alternate options. Veena Patil's courage deserves to be applauded. Veena World is the fasted built brand in our country.

Chitale's Bakarwadi, Gore brothers of Sangli's Bhadang, Lonavala's Maganlal Chikki or Diwadkar of Karjat's Vada Pav all these have sustained their brands year after year. Same taste, same standard. These ordinary appearing qualities have given them a strong place in the international markets, crossing national boundaries. These brands have survived over years on the strength of hard work, perseverance, marketing, and trust of the people. These are perfect examples of how even a small business can establish a brand, if done with loyalty and integrity.

Tata Group is the largest multinational conglomerate in India, which operates in more than 80 countries around the world. There is no need to explain separately the power of the Tata brand. Customers are ready to accept with blind eyes the quality of any product associated with Tata brand. The trust earned by the Tata's is incomparable. That is, this brand was built from the long and severe penance of the Tata Group. The masses of people have great faith in all products, from salt to motors, manufactured by Tata. The industrial empire of Tata has been erected on the basis of this trust-worthiness combined with integrity. The Tata brand has earned a special place in the mind of customers, due to the Tata Group leadership being insistent about merit, quality control, modernization and changing with the times.

Linked to the trust-worthiness the Tata name became the Tata brand. Trustworthiness and responsibility to the nation became relevant to the Tata name.

Brand is an idea linked to trustworthiness. Then the thought came forward that if this is codified then all the plus points of the company can be viewed at a glance. Accordingly, the use of a logo came into being. Tata had several companies. The brand of all the companies was not similar. Each company made a brand as it wanted. It was humorously told that "if all the Tata brands were to be displayed, it would cover all the walls of the Tata headquarters." Finally, Tata prepared a common symbol for all companies. One particular font was used for writing the name Tata. Then the English alphabet 'T' was drawn in a blue ellipse. This became the brand for all companies in the Tata Group. Ratan Tata himself stated, "We did not have a brand. Our brand used to be displayed in 15 to 20 symbols." Each company behaved as it wanted. Finally as per his own suggestion a common logo was prepared for all companies in the group.

Every company prepares a logo like this. The whole company is recognized by this one logo. The logo is very useful in pushing the said company into the mind of the people. Some people think that the brand is an advertisement in reaching the company's reputation to the people. The brand and logo go hand in hand. Hence, the decision on these should be well thought about, because this is permanent. It cannot be changed frequently. Hence, the company's name and logo should be decided thoughtfully. A word of a different kind could be effective, while selecting the name of a company. Such a word is easy to register. Also the word selected should be able to convey the meaning specifically. The meaning of this word should be commonly similar in all cultures. Many a time the name selected is somewhat similar to the name of a big, reputed company. Sometimes by miss-spelling an alphabet in the name, effort is made to seek a legal loophole. But it does not take long for people to see through this mischief. Once the cheating is exposed, the whole reputation of the company is mired. Hence, it is in one's own interest, not to attempt so.

The meaning of the name and logo is imprinted deeply in the mind of the people. A burning wick and the covering hand protecting it from the wind, this logo of Life Insurance Corporation of India creates a very positive image in the mind. Air India's logo 'Maharaja' suggests all the pride, impression, and kingly attributes of the air carrier. The child that depicted Murphy, the radio company had earlier become a darling of every home. The name and logo of the company should supplement each other. Even without the company's name, the company should be able to be identified by merely its logo. The company's name and logo have a big share in the branding of a company.

Even the world-class multi-national companies are incredibly cautious and sensitive about their brand. P&G the name that the company Procter and Gambel is known by, has sustained its brand for over one hundred and fifty years. This company started in America by two Britishers, William Procter and James Gamble, is a story of co-incidences like that you see in films. Both of them, who went to try their destiny in America, came together after marrying two real sisters. Initially, both were in the business of making candles. They started their company

Procter and Gamble on October 31, 1937. The company's beginning was rather shaky, but their destiny was so strong that they got a contract to supply candles and soap to the American military during the American civil war. That became the turning point of the company. The company's empire began expanding day by day after that. The company that started with only 80 employees, has one lakh employees today. The turnover of the company in 2012 was $83.68 billion. Procter and Gamble was included in the top 15 companies in the Fortune list's world ranking. The company has earned an economic power that could exert pressure on the whole world. If you consider the brand, it has earned a strength that any citizen of any nation in the world would bow to. It is clear that, a small household business of making candles, could grow into a behemoth like company, is the result of very hard striving for several decades. Every business has an identity. But every business cannot build a brand like this. None of the brands are made instantly. Your identity is determined by your distinctiveness in business. And on how you sustain this identity will depend on your brand. Brand in this respect is very significant.

Today, with just single letters, the brands of facebook, whatsapp, twitters, googles, instagram, etc. are very..

Every businessman should be prepared to put in that much effort if his business has to create a brand and it has to impress the mind of the mass of people. Veteran industrialist Shantanurao Kirloskar has ended his autobiography *Cactus and Roses* very psychologically. In his 79th year a friend asked him, "How are you?" He replied very casually, "I am very good. Even though the machine (body) has become old, it is working well.

Finally it is a 'Kirloskar' product only no!" In these words of Kirloskar lie hidden 'how a brand is significant.'

> *In this ever-changing society, the most powerful and enduring brands are built from the heart. They are real and sustainable. Their foundations are stronger because they are built with the strength of the human spirit, not an ad campaign. The companies that are lasting are those that are authentic.*
>
> —**Howard Schultz,** CEO of Starbucks

□

10

Rules and Laws

Our assets walk out of the door each evening.
We have to make sure that they come back the next morning.

—**Narayan Murthy,** Founder of Infosys

Business is directly related to money. The ultimate objective of any business is to create wealth only. Hence, the society considers industrialists or businessmen to be very rich people and mostly this is true too. It is clear that businessmen have money and barring few exceptions, the money is made by following all rules and laws. In a way, this wealth is the fruit of the industrialist's intelligence and years of hard work put in by him. There is a general assumption that industrialists and businessmen are thieves and they have accumulated wealth by squeezing the poor. But the real fact is totally different. These industrialists have spent several years in an air of stiff competition and extreme stress conditions. First, they have to study their sector. Then they have to collect some money and start a business properly. They have to foresee the plan for the next 25-30 years in their mind and take their steps. Without giving much thought to their home and family, they have to work very hard.

The childhood of any renowned businessmen of repute has been very ordinary. They attained success by struggling through very adverse situations at every step. It was very difficult to start a venture in pre-independence days. The intention of the British Government was not to allow growth of industry in India. Hence, their business policy was to throttle business and clip their wings. After independence in the initial period our industrial policy was decided as per the laws made by the Britishers. Hence, there were many obstacles on the path of starting an industry or business. Corrupt officials and the slow working bureaucracy created obstacles at every step before the industrialists. This policy of obstruction only made possible the causing of several industrialists to be disheartened. Government officials always got the opportunity to obstruct industrialists by misusing the Labor laws and the Factories Act. Government permits and registration were the readymade tools got by the officials. The permit-quota systems are the main obstructions for industrial development. The industrialist had to fight against the vested interest, enemies, and pave a path through all these obstacles and move ahead. Talking about his father, Dhirubhai Ambani, renowned businessman Mukesh Ambani used to always state, "Obstacles are not obstructions, but it is an opportunity. Obstacles compel you to carve a path, to combat and totally trounce it. One failure or so is an interval to prepare for the next leap. Only you should add more power to your effort in difficult times." Undoubtedly, this philosophy of Dhirubhai is an inspiration for everyone. Particularly, for those entering business for the first time and confronting a wave of obstacles every moment, this thought give tremendous energy of hope. Vested interest groups and individuals, while erecting anything, raise obstacles. If these obstacles are confronted with courage, they pass away. Not merely the new entrepreneur, but also the seasoned and renowned businessmen have to face these obstacles. Shantanurao Kirloskar has cited an experience in his autobiography. A senior minister in the State Government met Shantanurao Kirloskar. The minister told Kirloskar to reduce the cost of his oil engines to enable selling it at a lesser price. Kirloskar refused. He clearly told him that the price could not be reduced by maintaining the consistent quality of his engines. "If we have to reduce the price we will have to bring down the quality and life of the engine. We cannot do this," he said. He also told that if those who cannot afford our engines, they can buy other alternatives available in the market. Instead of trying to understand why his engines are costlier than others, he stressed that Kirloskar should bear in mind that he is getting orders due to a government scheme and hence should reduce the price. Kirloskar told him that this was the price in the whole country and he could not bring down the price for one State only. On this the minister arrogantly said, "By reducing the price for a year or so your company will not sink instantly." He not only alleged that Kirloskar was robbing the buyers, but also questioned him "Do you consider yourself bigger than the State?" He took upon himself that my reply insulted him. Finally, the concession announced by the government was not applicable to our engines. So buyers got no financial assistance to buy our engines. The minister's anger on Kirloskar lasted many days. After two years he lost his ministership and the ban on Kirloskar engines was lifted. From the above example, it is clear that globally reputed business group like the Kirloskars too could face obstacles in their profession and also how severe political pressure could also be exerted. In this case, Kirloskar stood his ground because he was fully justified. If your side is just, faultless, and lawful, you can confront any difficulty with a raised head, it is clear from this. There must have been several businessmen in Maharashtra and the whole of India, who have withstood corrupt government officials and greedy politicians. The motto of their business is to do their business with integrity and to follow all rules and laws. Capacity and skill can be earned in a business-profession; but fairness, integrity, and trust-worthiness have to be inbred. Subrato Bagchi, the co-founder and vice president of 'Mind Tree' in his book *Friendship with Professionalism* has given a very good example. In 2008, famous businessman Laxmi Mittal's Mittal Steel Company purchased the Arcelar Company in England. Arcelar was the biggest business house in the steel sector in Europe. He wanted to take the assistance of other companies to improve the cost-effectiveness, working methods, profit-related works. He called for applications from various companies for this work. These papers came to 'Mind Tree' too. 'Mind Tree' did not have the capacity to do the massive work of the mighty company like Arcelar. Vishal Gupta the European division chief of 'Mind Tree' was aware of this. In his offer to Arcelar, he clearly admitted that his company did not have the capacity to do all the work of that company. "But we have the heartfelt desire to do your work". Therefore, he requested in his application to be given the opportunity to do a part of their work.

On this, it was mentioned in the reply from Arcelor, "we found only one company to accept in fairness their own defects and limitations." Pleased with their fairness, he allocated the whole work to 'Mind Tree.' 'Mind Tree' actually got the whole work worth crores of rupees from Arcelar only because of their fairness and integrity. That is the strength in fairness and integrity. It is finally in everybody's interest that the directors of a company and employees follow every law. Directors of several companies unknowingly indulge in cheating in matters like that of income tax or sales-purchase and several other transactions. This cheating of theirs can be ignored once in a while. Just as the saying goes that truth can never die, these things will one day be exposed. And the individual will have to bear the fruits of his action. The wealth and name of those who disobey the law and behave illegally will be destroyed in a moment. The erected structure will be reduced to dust, only because of temptation. Many people might remember the Satyam scam that became famous a few years ago. Satyam Computers was an Indian company
that ranked fourth in software sector. The company's dealing ran into a few thousand crore rupees. It was proved that Mahalingam Raju, the founder and managing director of Satyam, only committed the scam. This scam was of ₹ 10,000 crore. Mahalingam Raju was arrested in this case. His massive empire collapsed as we watched. His reputation was tarnished. Sahara and many others are facing the same consequence. This means that a profession is successful if all laws and rules are followed in erecting the same. Any industrialist should set up his industry fearlessly. Business is done to create wealth and

earn money. But following all existing laws only, the said business should be erected. For this, all transactions related to the business should be transparent. There is a saying that the ferocious Brahma Rakshasa chases the fearful. But you have no reason to fear, if your dealing is very clear and perfect. Every industrialist should take care of some basic things. Therefore, do all things lawfully from the very beginning and avoid the illegal path totally. If you have a doubt of even the pettiest thing, seek legal advice and do not tread outside the legal frame. For this, all businesses should always seek advice from good lawyers. Many a time vested interests groups and sometimes competitive businessmen try to erect legal hurdles at every step. The legal hurdles do not last long, if your legal dealings are perfect. For this you should have a firm confidence. The other big hurdle in any business is that of government officials. These officials have the powers to issue various licenses required for business. Many greedy officials can hold up the licenses and hinder the businessman. Without being provoked at such times, the businessman should properly and practically keep trying by following the right path. One must also keep in mind that all officers are not like that.

Phone Call from a Bhai (Gangster)

Another element tormenting new and acclaimed businessmen is known as 'Bhai' (organised gangster). They are goons eyeing the money of businessmen. These goons, sometimes themselves and sometimes as a pawn of somebody else, threaten businessmen. Their straightforward intention is to extort money by threatening. They thrive if the businessmen fear them.

Their threats and demands keep increasing. Businessman may feel that the only way to silence them is to tamely give in to their demand. But this is not the last answer to the issue. As the torment of the goon goes on increasing. Also, these goons keep warning not to go to the police or anybody else, about this case, or will face severe consequences if he does that. Hence, new businessmen fear much. This they cannot tell anybody at home or elsewhere. Now the call from Bhai is not an out of this world event. But any new businessman receiving such a call is petrified. He cannot comprehend what to do or what not to do? Should he tell his wife and children? Should he inform his friends? Should he report it to the police? Many such issues torment him. Many people's mentality would be to wind up the business, feeling helpless in such a situation, and with frustrated feeling "I do not want this business nor have anything to do with that Bhai." But one should stay stable and strong in such a situation. One should take it as a part of life. One should have the discretion about whose help and to what extent one should take. In my opinion, it is best to go to the police. Some people also suspect that how could they be sure that the police (with exceptions) are not in league with the goons (Bhais) – If you cannot think of anything else, it is in your interest to resort to the police. Such a situation should be dealt by the businessman with a very cool mind and courageously. It is anytime better to go to the police at such times. For, because of this the threat is officially registered. The said businessman gets protection. Besides, the vast numerical strength of the police can take care of the said goon. The severity of the threat of the goon keeps increasing prior to the businessman going to the police. But the moment he comes to know that the police have been approached, the pressure of the goon is reduced to half. The businessman along with the help of the police should also have his own private security system in place. Keeping all entry points of the office under control, appointing security guards and using ultra-modern gadgets like CCTV are significant ways of avoiding any peril. By themselves behaving lawfully and doing everything within legal and moral framework, businessman should also be alert about other things too.

"The best way to predict the future is to create it."

—**Peter Drucker,** world renowned Management Guru

□

11

Social Responsibility

"Whatever has come from the people, should go back to the people in several times more measure."

—Jamshedji Tata

Azeem Premji, president of the world renowned company Wipro has a remarkable passion for education. His favorite hobby is to specially visit various schools to understand the actual condition of education there, by communicating with the teachers and students. He once went to a school in a remote village in Andhra Pradesh. He learnt that a girl in the VIII standard has been continuously absent since the last few days. Her friend informed that the girl's economic condition at home was not good and hence she could not come to school. Not only this, her friend revealed further, the girl's parents are trying to get her married. This pained Azeem Premji a great deal. His sensitive mind was deeply hurt at the thought of a girl forced to leave school due to poverty and the attempt to get her married, even though she is a minor, to avoid economic burden. He actually became restless at the very thought that how many boys-girls in India must be facing this situation. The only solution to this is that the education of every child must continue and they should get quality education. The thought that he should shoulder responsibility for this, did not allow him to be in peace. From this was born, 'Azeem Premji Foundation for Education.' Today, 21000 schools in 13 states of the country receive educational assistance from 'Azeem Premiji Foundation'. Azeem Premji has contributed 25 per cent of his income, about ₹ 12000 crore for this project.

Earning profits is the main objective of any business. It is true that no business can run without profits, but the greed for undue profits can be harmful to the whole business. Hence, every businessman should seriously decide as to what should fairly be his proportion of profit. Also, he should bear in mind that this profit is earned from the customers, that is from the community in which they live. It is humane to give back to the community that has provided them so much prosperity, in the spirit of expressing gratitude, by spending a part of the income earned for the welfare of society. Many industrialists and businessmen have realized this social responsibility. From this has emerged the concept of Corporate Social Responsibility (CSR). This concept existed in ancient times too. CSR could be verily defined as 'Voluntary Compliance of Social and Ecological Responsibility of Companies.'

Many cultures presume that any income is got, from the bounty of nature and the co-operation of the society. Ancient Indian culture has, time and again, expressed gratitude for this co-operation of nature and society. Every commandment in the Vedas bears witness to this. From, even the hermits should make only three *bhakris* (chappatis), of that one is for the cow, one for the guest and only one should be for self-consumption, it states. The idea of charity is inbred in every atom of the human being. The human being finds internal satisfaction and mental peace in very large measure when he donates a part of what he has.

In CSR, attempt has been made to give a somewhat disciplined shape to this emotion. A businessman William J. Beben was the first to present the concept of CSR in 1953. In 1990, a German company, German Betapharm effectively implemented it. Now this concept has started being implemented as a moral/legal duty. Some businesses have implemented this even before that. But now in recent times, various companies are taking up their share of this social responsibility in a systematic manner and with a specific objective. Many companies have given this social responsibility an equal importance accorded to their production. The reputation of the companies grew due to CSR. The companies experienced that it had a favorable effect on the customers and even the performance of the workers improved.

Azeem Premji expressed these very sentiments in his speech. Azeem Premji, the chairman of Wipro, ranks fourth among the richest people in India. He took charge of the affairs of Wipro at the age of 21. Today, Wipro is among the most reputed multi-national companies in India. Wipro's wealth is estimated to be about ₹ 1 lakh crore.

Azeem Premji realized that if the condition of our nation has to be changed, then we have to change the education system. For this, he prepared modern education in an easy and exciting language for students in remote rural regions of India. In 2010, he contributed

₹ 12000 crore from his income for the spread of this education. Inaugurating this project, he presented the concept of corporate social responsibility in a very clear and effective manner in his speech. He had then said, "I strongly believe that those of us who are privileged to have wealth should contribute significantly to try and create a better world for the millions who are far less privileged."

He spoke the very principle exhorted in our Upanishads, "May everybody be happy, May everybody be free from diseases. May everybody have good tidings? May none fall on evil days."

In Azeem Premji's opinion, the government cannot do everything. Our responsibility (duty) should be as much as our rights and success. CSR makes the workers mentally aware of their responsibility, thereby improving their performance and profits of the company.

Just as the understanding of the company's responsibility grew, so also the CSR sentiments grew. The example of 'Ford Foundation' in America is well known around the world. The Ford brothers established this organization in 1936. This work started with $25000. Financial assistance is provided from this fund for economic empowerment, education, human rights, protection of democracy, art, and other creative pursuits. This work gradually kept growing. Today the Foundation spends $90 billion (about ₹ 5,40,000 crore) on this work.

In India, the reputed Tata and Birla Groups implement CSR very effectively. Both of them have established independent Foundations and provide assistance on a very large scale to workers and needy children from this.

The Tata Cancer Research Institute, run on this same role, has carved a special place in the mind of all Indians. Due to the special interest, of Ratan Tata, the former president of the Tata Group and Shrimati Rajeshri Birla of Birla Business Group, in CSR work, CSR was given priority in both the industry groups.

Tata's founded leading educational institutes like Tata Institute of Fundamental Research (TIFR) Mumbai, Tata Institute of Social Sciences (TISS), Mumbai, Indian Institute of Science (IISC), Bengaluru, etc. The Birla organization too has weaved a network of CSR all over India like the Birla Institute of Technology (BITS), Pilani.

CSR can be implemented not only by big business groups or those with turnover of crores of rupees alone. If businessmen desire, then in their own way, they can implement such social welfare schemes. Many small companies have set such examples. Vilasrao Gavkar, director of Thane's 'Swami Samarth Udyog Group', a small-scale industry, has set an ideal example of CSR by a small company. He started the business of carting goods in his tempo in his 30s. Slowly, he started a chemist shop. In a short span, he grew his business considerably on the strength of his integrity and fairness. But on the advice of a Guru he met, he changed his business from a chemist shop to selling medicines without any profit. Today also, his customers can get medicines at a lesser price. With social welfare consciousness many small businessman can do big work.

Nirmala Girish Kandalgaonkar, who hailed from Aurangabad and settled in Pune, established her whole business with a CSR sentiment. She prepared a plant to make earthworm manure from household waste and food waste. Improving on that she added a plant to generate gas and later, electricity. She discovered a formula to convert this on a larger scale to provide cooking gas and electricity for the whole village. With the electricity from this plant, she could operate an electric crematorium. To publicize her plant, she addressed meeting of villagers in many villages. She explained to them the structure of the plant. She trusts that this will give employment to the garbage collectors and gas and electricity to the village. She implemented this successfully in many villages. Nirmalatai taught the female workers in a village like Chandrapur to ride a bicycle. These women therefore began to collect garbage at a faster pace. Today Nirmala Kandalgaonkar's plant is operational in many villages in Maharashtra. This middle-class woman, Nirmala Kandalgaonkar's 'Vivam Udyog Group' business is an ideal example of corporate social responsibility. She is an advisor to several municipal corporations and municipalities on waste management. Even though the objective of any business is to earn profits, business should bear society in mind while distributing profits. It is essential that on humanitarian grounds some portion of the profit should be spent for the society. If we do this, we can easily fulfill our duty towards society.

Even if a company has to spend some amount for CSR, ultimately it is profitable to the company. Azeem Premji has said just that and he proved it too. Dr. Devi Shetty, a renowned doctor of Bengaluru's Narayan Hridayalaya brought out this fact very clearly before the world. This is a one thousand beds hospital. 600 heart operations are done every week in this hospital. This hospital is run in the spirit of 'service to mankind is service to God.' The hospital has also established a principle that instead of earning more profits by chasing money, we can increase the volume of our work and earn more profits. The cost of the operation in this hospital is normally $2000 (₹ 1 lakh 20 thousand). For the same operation in America, the cost of the operation would come to $1 lakh (₹ 60 lakh). That means there is big difference in the expense for this in both the countries. In spite of this, the proportion of the Narayan Hridayalaya doctors' profit is 7.7 percent. But the doctors in America, though charging high profits, earn only 6.9 percent. Keeping social service in mind, behaving so, yet the profit share is not reduced. Is this not clear from this?

Responsibility about the society should be in the mind of the concerned individual only. The Tata Industries Group, with a 140 years tradition, never allowed the thought of social responsibility to be out of sight. The Tata tradition of placing economic success second only to fulfilling social objectives continues even today. The Tata Group has considered it their objective to build new hope on the basis of building values in society. The Tata Group does not consider, obtaining the highest place in its selected market, as its objective. They stress on building high values. Hence the word 'trust' has the highest value in the group. The words, 'I too have eaten the salt of this nation,' therefore come spontaneously, in the advertisement of Tata Salt. Tata lays more stress on giving service to the people, rather than capturing the market. Tata has used the slogan 'wake up' in the Tata tea advertisement. The same sentiment lies behind this too.

The story of Titan Watch Industries started by Tata Industry Group and Tamil Nadu Industrial Development

Corporation is very expressive. This company was established in 1985 and the production commenced in 1987 from Hosur in Tamil Nadu, where the factory was erected. Tatas ardently believed that local talent emerges from the region where the factory is set up. The issue of, where to bring workers from, came up while starting the watch factory. Tata could have easily brought in skilled workers from Bengaluru or Chennai. But they gave priority to local talent. They selected 480 people from Hosur itself. They were given the required training. The Titan Company grew on their skill and hard work. This company gave employment to thousands of workers in Tamil Nadu. Three factories of Titan came up in Takayya Hosur region only. The company achieved a world record of manufacturing the slimmest, waterproof watches. Is this not a social responsibility fulfilled by the Tatas that a remote, almost an unheard village, was catapulted to the global map?

When Tata Finance Company collapsed in 2003, Tatas lost ₹ 500 crore. But Tatas returned every paisa of the investors. Is this not an example of social responsibility that care was taken that the community that reposed faith on them should not be put to the minutest loss because of them?

Tatas established the Indian Institute of Science in Bengaluru to conduct basic research in the field of science. Jamshetji Tata passed away in 1904. Prior to his death, he willed one-third of his property to assist this institute. The sentiment behind this was that "whatever came from the people should be returned to them manifold."

Dhirubhai Ambani fairly admits "I spent all my time in business. Hence, I did not get time for social work." But he clarifies immediately after, "giving the best product at a cheaper price is my social responsibility."

Tatas have set up an ideal of social responsibility at Jamshedpur. An organization called 'Tata Steel Rural Development Society' has been established there. Nearly 800 villages in Jharkhand and Orissa are benefitted by various schemes of this society. This organization conducts several social activities like free health services, education, financial assistance to dig wells, mobile dispensary, family planning, AIDS counseling and guidance, assistance and guidance to farmers to increase productivity and so many other activities, also sports facilities, cleanliness, sewage disposal and driving classes too.

The efforts of Kirloskar, for a clean, beautiful and green Pune, are known to all. The Kirloskar Group conducts 'ideal school' competition to promote competition for merit in schools. This competition and the encouragement that the schools get should be considered as a part of Kirloskar Industry Group's social responsibility.

Jamshedji's basic viewpoint is at the root of this concept. Jamshedji had stated, 'It is my responsibility that for those of my countrymen, who are not as privileged as me, I should constantly strive to provide a favorable environment."

"Wealth is sometimes with one person and sometimes with the other. We are only trustees of the wealth with us, ultimately the whole wealth belongs to the society only."

—Mahatma Gandhi

□

12

Disaster Prevention

Between my past, the present and the future, there is one common factor:
Relationship and Trust. This is the foundation of our growth.

—**Dhirubhai Ambani,** Founder of Reliance

The sentiment of social responsibility should be inherent in any business. Many renowned businessmen have effectively implemented this concept. It is generally accepted that since money earned in business has come from the society and the hard work of employees and workers, business should shoulder its responsibility for their welfare. At the same time, it is necessary to take care in any business that no harm is caused to society and the life of the workers too is not in peril. It is also necessary in any business to take care to prevent disaster so that no harm is caused to society. An effective system should be put in place, in such business, to protect from sudden disasters. In big industries these days, the employees are quite large in number. Hence, in these conditions a small disaster too can cause damage in large proportion. Hence, it is obligatory to seriously think about disaster prevention and with reference to that, disaster management.

There are two types of mishaps – natural disasters and accidents. There is always a possibility of accidents in big industries. Mishaps can be caused by fire, gas, and chemical leaks or failure of systems. In this, the probability of fire and gas leaks is more. To ensure minimum damage many schemes are implemented on a war footing. Prevention, preparedness, rescue, relief, and rehabilitation are the five main stages of disaster prevention. Many companies take complete care of all these five steps. Many schemes are made. Employees are given training and many times mock drills are held regarding this.

In various factories mishaps caused by fire are very frequent. Hence, there is the highest need to adopt modern fire prevention measures. A properly working fire alarm system to warn employees is needed. The main entrance of the factory should be sufficiently wide. This will enable fire brigade vehicles and ambulances to enter easily. Many factories were established away from residential areas. Gradually, the residences multiplied and a situation of the factories being in the midst of residences was created. In such a situation, factories should consider the safety of vehicles too.

What big damage one mishap can inflict, can be gauged from the Bhopal tragedy in the Union Carbide gas leak mishap. This gas leak claimed the life of hundreds of workers/citizens and thousands of others affected, suffered permanent disability. The ill-effects are being borne by many even today. Such mishaps can occur in chemical factories any time. Hence, precautions should be taken on a war footing.

Several new developments are taking place about equipments used for disaster management. Taking note of these regularly, these equipments should be incorporated in the factory's system from time to time. FICCI has got many types of equipment made by DRDO. In this, there is an equipment called 'Sanjeevani.' In this equipment, there are sensors that can detect breathing under the debris in a building collapse mishap. A multi-purpose stretcher that can float on water has also been made. A multi-purpose rescue kit has been made by the 'Think Health' organization. Factories should avail the use of such kinds of new research. Training in the use of these new equipments should also be given to the workers and employees.

In every industry, there is an independent department for disaster prevention. This department keeps watch on the kinds of dangers. This department has to do various kinds of work like maintaining modern fire system in the industry, training employees, registering the blood group of the employees, keeping important phone numbers, and other essential information in such a place that employees can get it easily in an emergency, doing preparatory work in order to source assistance at the earliest from outside and other works.

Whether the business/factory is big or small, the management has to erect the disaster prevention system. In modern times, management is very much aware about this. The disaster preventive measures have to be taken to prevent any mishap in the factory and to prevent any effect on citizens in the vicinity because of the factory.

Healthcare

Businessmen should take care of their own mental and physical health. Businessmen have to fight on all fronts. Businessman is dragged into taking flawless decisions, raising capital, sourcing materials and equipment, selecting employees, calculating profit-loss, need to survive in competition and discovering new sectors. The word 'Rest' is wiped off from his daily schedule. New problems emerge every moment. Many issues have to be sorted out. Struggling at every step, he has to maintain consistent pace of progress. He cannot devote enough time for his family. He totally neglects his own health through this hectic schedule. More than his physical strain, it is the mental stress that tires him more.

Taking all this into consideration, any businessman should take due care of his health. Keeping control on his food intake, he should observe required discipline in his daily life. Also allocating a fixed time, he should rest also. Several times, change in work is also like a form of rest. Therefore, businessmen should find recreation in some work of their liking. He can find his lost relaxation in a hobby like music, games, reading or gardening.

How much ever a man filled with hope keeps working, he will feel tired at some point of time. He needs rest at that time. His body keeps giving him signals from time to time. Taking note of these signals, he should take proper rest. Do not miss health signals, and if you neglect this, then many working days may go waste. Businessmen should keep their body fit with games or exercise. They have to maintain their health properly by doing all the necessary investigations from time to time. They should take care of their mental health by paying full attention to their family. If they give sufficient time for the family, then the environment in the home can be enthusiastic and joyful.

It is necessary for businessmen to take care of their own health. Healthcare, from all viewpoints, is the foundation for running a business smoothly. Due to this, your and the business downtime will be reduced to the minimum.

Even if the businessman has flung himself into his work, then he should not forget his family. He should reserve sometime every week for the family. Just as it is true that he should not carry any of his domestic work to the office, it is also equally true that he should not carry any of his official work to his home. He should not allow his stressful work to impact the family atmosphere at home. On returning home, once he crosses the threshold, he should forget business, it should be home and only home.

"You ruin your health to earn more and more and then you spend more and more to recover your health."

□

13

Stress-free Life

"If you don't build your dream, someone else will hire you to help them build theirs."

—Dhirubhai Ambani, Founder of Reliance

'We ruin our health to earn more and more. Later on we spend more and more to recover health', is the normal observation. Stress-free life is the master key to sound health and mental peace. Earning profit or making wealth is the very purpose of any business and it should be so. But businessmen should also be balanced about profits. Every business has its own pace. The businessman's skill lies in taking care of this pace, sustaining it and making a planned growth. Sometimes, in the greed for wealth, businessmen forget values. Then unfair means are adopted. In this, sometimes you do get success but it does not last longer. If business is run at the right pace, then right profit is made at the right time. When a business or businessman suddenly, in an unnatural way, grows big, then, it is not growth, it should be understood as a swelling. The graph of a business that grows suddenly at such a magical pace, collapses too at the same pace. Hence, it is in one's own interest to progress at a tolerable pace rather than face the dangers of such rise and fall and bear such shocks. For this, businessmen should have self-control. For this self-restraint, his mind has to be spiritually inclined. No one can be happy by making others unhappy. If you sow happiness, then only you reap happiness. Spirituality is when human beings think of other beings in a humanitarian way. The spirituality of businessmen is to do business in a fair manner and ultimately achieve the welfare of the community. When you do business based on spirituality you can run a long race and accomplish your own interest and thereby of the society and the nation. Aspirations and competition build stress in the mind, and an individual takes out this stress on others. The boss takes this stress out on to his junior. This goes on downward and finally the last individual takes out that anger on his family. This causes increase in family strife. A businessman should try to lead a stress-free life to avoid all these. Life can be stress-free only by living a fair life.

Court Cases and Tax Raids

Since business is directly related to wealth and the social superiority that comes from wealth, businessmen many a time provoke the ire of the people. At the same time envious people from various classes adopt a policy of obstruction. Several decades ago that is prior to India adopting the open market policy, there was the 'permit-quota' rule in India. Several hurdles were put in the way, if anyone wanted to start a new business. The hurdles of permissions were particularly put at every step. Permission had to be sought for everything and these would take many days to get. You had to approach the concerned officers several times. Big industrialists like Tata, Birla, Ambani, Narayan Murthy have faced this difficulty in the matter of permits. Ministers used to decide on policy matters of big industries and these industrialists have to face the brunt of the minister's mind and mood. People with the authority to issue permits are well versed in creating obstacles. But all officers are not like that. Many are sticklers to the law and behave objectively. But the sticklers to the law are not hurdles to those who follow the rules. Hence, every businessman should first be very strict about following rules himself. He should be firm about not doing anything illegal or violate any rule. Businessmen should follow every rule to the word, in matters of the factory land, production permits, recruitment of employees and sale of produced products and taxes on the same. If they follow this rule, pay all taxes properly from time to time, no one can obstruct them. However, corrupt a government official may be, he cannot do anything against anyone who follow the rules. Businessmen should take care, to see that they do not break any laws and all their actions should be within the legal framework, to avoid the fear of bribe and losses.

Just as hurdles are put in business in the matter of permits, vested interests try to put obstacles on various issues of legal points. In this mainly it is the competitors in the same field. These legal hurdles begin from the very point of buying land itself. Objections are raised for construction. Issues like environment or public peace are deliberately raised. Cases are filed in the court on small, small issues. One more class of black mailers has recently emerged. This class is called RTI activist. Again, not all are like that. But some of them are professional RTI activists. They have no other job. They keep filing RTI applications and seek information. It is their bread and butter. I feel, there is a flaw in the RTI Act that the information should only be given when the concerned activist or applicant can prove that he/she is affected party. This will reduce black mailing. The act is good, but being misused by many. This misuse should be stopped. Most of the time, the complainant is prone to prolong the cases only. If the businessmen have followed the rules and remained in the legal framework, then they have no reason to fear such cases. They will win ultimately. Hence, businessmen should not fear such judicial lawsuit brokers and also not lose their composure. They should take legal advice every time and be prepared to fight it out. However, they should always be alert about such litigations.

Any legal matter should be handled seriously. Any case, be it big or small, should be settled in the nick of time. Taking the help of expert lawyers for this is essential. Ignoring legal issues could make matters worse in no time. Sometimes there is the peril of your lawyer being managed. Therefore, businessmen while reposing full faith on their lawyers, should also be careful about them. Judicial cases are, in a way, war only. If businessmen want to play it with the same resolve, then they should be aware of all the (legal) armory used in it. Civil matters remain pending for years. Such cases are very rarely settled in the court. These cases are mostly filed to pressurize the people concerned and to obstruct them. Neither the complainants nor their lawyers are interested in getting judgment in the case. Hence, effort should be made to settle these cases out of court. Considering the strength of specific cases, attempt to compromise and arrive at an 'out of court settlement' should be made. Time and money are saved in this. Also mental stress is avoided. Businessmen should take a decision with discretion on this. But the time has to come for every settlement. Incubation period is required. So, sufficient patience should be shown. Apart from the hurdles at the government level and litigation filed by vested interests, there is one more trial by fire that businessmen have to undergo.

Unable to get anything from businessmen who follow the law strictly and act within the legal framework, another attempt to exhaust them is made through one more way. This way is getting a raid on them. This is a very effective weapon in the hands of government officials. This weapon is used to teach a lesson to big industrialists or to make them tow their line. These raids are very tormenting from any businessman's point of view. In this, he is maligned much. Everyone starts looking at him with suspicion. Raids are conducted at the same time at his main office, other offices, and houses of relatives, godowns, showrooms and all premises concerning him. Apart from being maligned during the period, all transactions too come to a standstill. Most of the times, the objective is revenge or arrogance to make the businessman dance to their tunes. Recently, it has come to the knowledge that the Income-tax officers even use the coercing methods, which include physical assault on the businessmen. A businessman cannot verify the correctness of this information as it is only a murmur and not a outspoken statement. Here you must keep one thing in mind, and it is to be understood that raids, survey, search, seizure and other such kinds are a part of business. Do not let disgrace, about this or any such sentiment, come in your mind? Such raids are attempts to put pressure and bring businessmen to submission. If you remain quiet and unaffected, maintaining restrain, then not much damage will be caused. Freezing bank accounts are done in exceptional cases. Raids run for 2-3 days. If you keep your mind unperturbed, you will not suffer from mental agony. They intend to make you suffer so and if you suffer so, they are successful. You should not allow that, to happen. It is not that if you are clean and behave lawfully, you will not face this difficulty.

Most of the laws are of the British period. Hence, they serve the interests of the rulers only. Government officials are proficient in picking up one or the other flaws and harassing businessmen. Ultimately, there is a complete legal settlement for everything. The policy of only obstructing businessmen was adopted during the tenure of some ministers whose head was filled with ideas of economic cleansing. Hence, several businessmen were raided. Even Tatas, who insist on obeying the law, too have borne the brunt of these raids. Raids were conducted on the Kirloskar Group of Industries during the lifetime of Shantanurao Kirloskar. With such an attitude a raid was conducted on the business of P.N. Gadgil, who was known all over the country for his integrity. The bank's transaction was closed for 4-5 days during the very festival period. Does the thought ever rise in the mind of those who order the raid and those who implement the orders that due to their raids, the businessmen or professionals are permanently maligned? The reputation earned by businessmen through working very hard without rest for several years can be reduced to dust by that one raid.

Hence, it should be ascertained once, how many raids were based on true information and how many raids were conducted vindictively and how much has been recovered from these raids. Of this, tax evasion raids are more suspect and impractical. Factually, businessmen do pay taxes. The government has a right to scrutinize them. Government can get information from the returns filed by them. If the government wants to make further enquiry about this, a squad of officials can do this in a peaceful manner anytime. For this it is not fitting to stop all transactions of businessmen and create an atmosphere of making them look like criminals, even before any allegation is proved. In the present times, computers can be used for this very effectively. All financial transactions can be scrutinized with the help of computers. After the tax raids, most concerned individuals have been found to be innocent. There may be irregularities about taxes, many a time. That does not qualify it as a crime. The government can have no right to defame a businessman till the crime is proved to be of a very serious nature. Hence, raids being conducted merely on suspicion should be stopped. Rather the policy on raids should be reviewed.

A businessman is inclined to correct a mistake made by him inadvertently. For this it cannot be an ideal government procedure to defame the businessman and cause him heavy financial losses till the raid procedure is completed. Basically, taxation should be regularly reviewed and made more practical. Only when taxation is impractical, there is a tendency to evade it. Business profits are normally in the range of 10 to 15 per cent.

Tax brackets should be in this range. This tax collection should not be made on the presumption that businessmen are criminals. Businessman being creators of national wealth, protecting their reputation itself is protecting the nation's reputation. The harassment of businessmen and professionals merely on suspicion should be stopped.

Raids on businessmen should not be conducted without definite grounds. These raids are used to blackmail businessmen several times. These raids are used as a weapon. Raids do not increase the government's revenue. On the other hand, business suffers a big setback.

One more aspect of tax collection should be given attention to. It is understood that out of the total tax collected, major portion is spent on the collection manpower and its machinery. Then what is the use of tax collection? Is it for the benefit of the tax collecting manpower alone? Just think of a reduced tax slab and payment or recovery mode other that the present one, say online and voluntary. It may be more economical to the government. Or think of an alternative to all the taxes by way of incorporating the transaction tax-like instrument and do away with all the taxes.

To avoid tax raids, the scrutiny of accounts should be made more accurate. A rule can be made to make online submission of accounts, every three months, compulsory. If the nation has to develop, the relations between the government and the business world should be cordial. If the policies and laws are oppressive then there will be disappointment in the business world. At the same time, it should also be noted that if the laws are followed and all taxes paid, then business can be run successfully and profitably. Some people feel that to be a businessman or a factory owner, one has to resort to various unfair practices and evade taxes. But people indulging in such evasions can never be happy. They cannot develop the business properly under constant pressure. But those businessmen, who follow the laws and pay all taxes properly develop themselves as also the nation. The nation progresses with citizens paying these taxes. One cannot find a single example of any tax-evading businessman grown big. It is in the interest of the nation that businessmen are sincere and the government too not is vindictive.

All the departments have the three kinds of measures, viz. survey, search, and raid. In survey, there is only the part of surveying while in search the scrutiny of documents and prying is done. In these the transactions are not affected, but in raids transactions are stopped.

The government is run on the taxpayer's money. So taxpayers are the owners. Hence, the right of servants to raid the owners should be withdrawn. Even business organizations should demand and make attempts to bring a ban forever on such raids. The business organizations do not seem to be doing this. The Central and State Governments should prepare a favorable atmosphere for business.

People are definitely a company's greatest assets. It doesn't make any difference whether the product is cars or cosmetics. The company is as good as the people it keeps.

—**Mary Kay Ash,** Founder of Mary Kay Cosmetics

□

14

Budget, Planning and Growth

"Doers get to the top of the oak by climbing it. Dreamers sit on an acorn."

Budget, planning, and growth, i.e. finance, planning, and development are the three key points of any business. Inspired with a goal, doing many things, at a specified pace is known as business. For this the work jurisdiction has to be decided. For any businessman the first thing to decide is the work location. Varied and mutually divergent things may not be able to be gathered at the same time. Hence, without determining the work location, a businessman cannot proceed even a step further. The company's chief who selects the work location should be very clever. It is not possible for one person to manufacture T.V., household appliances and cloth at the same time. Hence, he has to first decide what exactly he wants to do. Instead of running for different things, it is important to manufacture one thing of best quality and maintain the quality, no matter how much the quantity increases. Only such business becomes famous. Singer sewing machines and Usha fans, with a tradition of several years, are popular even today. Their quality is inherent in their very name. Businessmen should enter that field with the understanding that the said field is meant for them only. Any businessman can find his field of work anywhere, may be in his vicinity too. It is necessary to work consistently and keep producing after deciding to do business in any field.

After starting production, stagnation will set in if the same product is produced over the years. Hence, constant research should be done to improve the quality and innovate the product. Over a period of time, necessary changes should be made. For this newer techniques should be beneficially used. The process of production should be changed as the need arises. New discoveries and facilities of science and technology should be used. Cloth made by handloom earlier, came to be manufactured by power looms. Then, came the textile mills. This technological progress made a lot of difference. More began to be produced in less time. World markets became accessible to all due to better transport facilities. Hence, presently it is the era of 'mass production.' But in this era too, the demand remains consistent if production is maintained in a particular way and particular quality. The Paithani sari of Yewla in Nasik district of Maharashtra has retained its dominance even today. New methods should be used to develop the product, increase production speed, and to produce on a large scale. The yearning for innovation should be in the mind and eyes of the businessman constantly. Also, take care to see that your working method is fast and flawless. People will use a thing only if they are sure about it. People will board a bus only if they are sure that it will reach them (to their destination) safely and on time. Once they are sure, people will ask for the same product again and again.

If you have to retain customers of your product then you have to ensure the quality of your product. But you must also keep raising the quality of the product constantly. You have to create a network of sellers to reach your produced goods to the market. Measuring the market economics of demand and supply, keeping the flow of your quality products supply constant is, what is running a business successfully. This is a penance for a long time. Perfect planning is its foundation.

Planning

A Sanskrit verse 'Yojakstatra Durlabh' states that many things in the world can be done easily, only the organizer or the leader is rare. The same can be said about business. Any individual can be a good organizer, when he plans in a proper manner. A draft plan should be ready before starting business. Starting any business in a way is like building a replica of universe. A businessman has to pay heed to things. It is said that this is not the work of any Tom, Dick or Harry. Prior to realizing any idea practically it should be conceptualized in the mind. It is the same about business too. The idea of any business is first conceptualized in the mind of the businessman. But that is not enough. Before actually starting the business, the draft plan should be ready on paper. This may be called the 'blueprint' of the business. Before actually starting a business, planning of this kind is very essential. The businessman will get an idea about, what he actually wants to do, due to such planning. He will be able to co-ordinate his resources, machinery, efficiency, and objective. Even if he has a big objective in his mind, he has to take steps only after estimating the resources with him. To achieve his objective he will be able to decide only when he knows, what will be the efficiency required and what system will be required for that. He will be able to estimate the expenses and income. In planning, the maximum importance is given to financial mattes. The income sources have to be considered. What will be the share of income to be given for varied things, will have to be decided. You have to also estimate in what proportion and what ways the invested money will be earned back. No builder will start constructing a building without making a plan/design of the house. So also a businessman cannot start actual work without making a draft plan. It is said at times that if one waits for everything to fall in place then actual work will never start. But he will have to figure out what things he will have to gather.

A draft plan, in a way, is like the budget estimate of the country. He, who presents the budget, has to determine how much money and resources he has, what are his needs and how much will he have to spend for these. The planning for business is also like this. Even if the budget is presented, it can be changed as per the need. But basically if there is no budget, then how can the direction and pace of work be known? A businessman will have to raise money from others for his proposed business. Only after looking at the draft plan of the business, any investor will think of investing in it. From this draft plan only, he can study the stages of development.

Anyone can know the size and shape of the business by seeing the draft plan. In that, the objective of the business, the products created by it, service, the distinctiveness of the product, probable costumers, competitors, condition of the product, condition of the market, estimate of expenditure, cost of things, money required to sustain the business for some years, facilities given to employees, disaster management, number of employees, marketing for long-term, a picture of all these can be clear in this draft plan. Even a businessman can determine the direction of development by using this plan. Based on the draft plan, the businessman can discuss with various groups every time. Changes in the draft plan can be made as per suddenly emerging situations.

In this draft, planning does have an importance in the erection of a business. But at the same time the planning for expenditure is also very important. In this, the purchase of plant and machinery, provision for paying taxes, expenditure on marketing and advertising and many other issues are included. Since the draft is not actually executed as it is, many a time the estimates change. But since the basic estimates are done, the change does not have much adverse effect.

Any business is started with a projection for the next fifteen years. From that point of view, every businessman wants his business to be of a long run. For this, the progress of the business will be possible if the draft plan of the business is finalized and the working proceeds in accordance with it. For this, the planning of any business in the very beginning is most important. Planning has to be micro planning for the short term and macro planning for the long term.

Capital Raising and Management

After the draft plan is made, the first question that arises, is that of Capital. In a way money is the breath of any planning. Without money any planning could be worthless. Rather, how to raise money constitutes the major part of planning. Without capital in hand, no concept can be materialized. Hence, businessman should give thought, as to how to raise capital. A businessman cannot raise all the money required for a business on his own. That is he cannot raise all the money of his own. This means that he has to raise this capital in various ways and from others.

Banks are a big source for raising capital for the businessman. Several banks give loans to new businessmen under various schemes. The government too gives loan through financial institutions. Raising loans in such a proper way is the best way for erecting a business. The interest rates of such institutions are also not very harsh. Only the possibility, of getting the total required capital from banks and finance institution, is less. You need to have some seed capital. At such a time, businessmen have to raise this capital from private investors. Several investors are willing to invest in various businesses. While taking financial assistance from such investors, a businessman should take help after properly assessing them. He should take precaution to see that he will not have to pay exorbitant interest. The investors ask for a big share of profits, many a time. Businessmen should be careful even at such a time. Businessmen should take care that the investors do not interfere in their business. After the investor has checked the business scheme completely, if he finds out what he is going to do, then he will not interfere in the business frequently. The businessmen should assess the sources properly and then only accept the money they are getting. Selecting the right investor and getting capital from him is the most important part of businessmen's financial planning.

While setting the economic structure of the business, the finance department should be exceptional. Hence, businessmen should take care to give the best accountants, auditors, lawyers, and employees to the accounts department. Businessmen should keep close watch on the income and outgoings of their business. They should also see whether sufficient funds are made available for essentials and if funds are maintained as reserve for any calamity.

Paying employee's salary on time, making petty and daily purchases properly, paying all taxes and installments in time, keeping control on advertisement expenditure, all these come within the ambit of financial management. It has also to be seen, as to what the company's loan is and whether the installments for repayment are being paid properly.

Payment of taxes is an important issue. If proper attention is not paid to this, then businessmen may have to repent. Penalty too has to be paid if taxes are not paid on time. And many times it leads to facing judicial litigation. They should understand all rules regarding taxation. Rather, to handle issues regarding taxation, any business should have an independent system. Like taxation, there should also be an accounting system that will suit the size and style of your business. For this, all ultra modern software should be used. A chartered accountant, tax consultant, and company secretary are all needed.

The chief accounts officer is responsible for all the financial management. This is a very responsible job. Hence, a very efficient officer should be appointed to this post. The accounts officer should be appointed on a good salary. Even if a larger amount of money has to be spent on this officer, it is an investment for the company. From this alone, the balance sheet of a company shows improvement.

Financial management is the system that gathers capital and keeps watch on its utilization. Neglecting this department could end up in loss and disaster.

Growth and Development of Business

Ultimately, growth and development are the soul of business. If business does not grow or it does not develop, then stagnation will set in the business and in a few years it will close down. The growth and development of business depends upon the profit of the business. Any business has to be conducted for profits. Only if attention is paid to profits, progress is possible. 'I do not want profits', is a sentiment expressed merely to show or express on the surface. Business cannot function with this thought. Hence, businessmen should constantly think of the growth and development of their business. Even service projects should function profitably, only then will it progress. The beginning of any business is always done on a small scale. Tata, Birla, Ambani, Kirloskar created an empire but their starting was from such small business only. Tatas have companies in more than eighty countries today. There is nothing in our daily life from the morning tea to going to sleep that is not related to the Tatas. It is indeed a test of intellectual efficiency to manage an industrial group that has a turnover running into thousands of crores and keeps consistently growing. Businessmen of such intellect and efficiency are the real capital of the nation, as wealth flows from their efforts.

Success cannot evade those businessmen who think of growth and development round the clock with assistance from proper planning and good management. The success saga of any businessman will reiterate this truth, again and again.

"American roads are good not because America is rich, but America is rich because American roads are good."

—Henry Ford

□

15

Marketing

"Marketing is the engine of a company. Speed of the engine is the speed of the train."

Marketing is the foundation of sales management. Any product, however good it may be, will be useless if there is no proper sales and distribution facility. As it will then not reach the customers. Hence, for any business, there should be a marketing system and it should be vigilant. It is most mandatory for the marketing team to have a proper study of the market. The team should have the sensitivity to immediately register even the minutest change in the market's rise and fall. The marketing team's main work is to impress the company's product in the mind of the common people, but along with, the team also has to reach the reaction of the market to the manufacturer/management. The members of this team, therefore, have to care for even the slightest note emanating in the market about the product. They have to have the sensitivity and alertness to catch this minute note. The team should also have the capacity to instantly analyze this minute reaction in the market. Doing market survey constantly and analyzing that information is an important formula of marketing.

The image and reputation of the product depend on the hard work of this team. This team's main work is to go to the big purchasers and explain the usefulness and quality of the company's product.

But while doing this, integrity and honesty should be the foundation of any marketing strategy. You may taste momentary success by false means, but that is not real. There is no other effective tool other than honesty for long-term success. The marketing manager should prepare his scheme and policy, keeping this integrity in mind.

The scope of the market has widened very much in the present times. Since long the market has extended beyond the local and national limits. The modern market has become global in the true sense. Hence, it has become impossible for small and developing nations to secure their market through artificial sanctions. It will ultimately be a loss for those nations, who think that in this competition of globalization they can remain aloof from others and move on their own. In this atmosphere all business will have to try hard to not to be isolated. The biggest responsibility of this lies with the marketing department. Whether the business is big or small, or of any nature, yet these new challenges have to be handled by the marketing department. For, ultimately they only are in direct contact with the market.

In modern times, customers have several alternatives since the competitive companies for any product have increased. They know all the details of everything since the media has reached every home. They easily get information of comparative prices. International products have flooded the market in competition with domestic products. Customers have become more selective since they have detailed information of alternative products and can order any product from any part of the world. In a way, the market has become a consumers' market or buyers' market.

The manufacturer or those in charge of the marketing department should have information of all things including consumer's economic status, their lifestyle, alternative products available, local environment, local laws, etc. The marketing team has to constantly visit various places in the country and abroad to get the feel of the market. They have to be in touch with agents in India and abroad, all the time. Hence, the employees working in the marketing department should be smart, agile, effective personality, good and clear communicator in different languages, with professional and technical knowledge and healthy from the physical and mental point of view. Such a kind of modern marketing department will guarantee success of any business.

A marketing department has to pay heed to the following points:

1. Prepare a marketing policy as per the objectives of the company.
2. Examine the policy regularly to keep the business progressive.
3. Study the environment of markets in the country and abroad.
4. Find out what changes can be introduced in the present product.
5. Investigate the possibility of new products.

6. Consider the possibility of imports for growth in business.
7. Find more new markets.
8. Create an image and reputation of the company in the mind of the customers.
9. Give feedback of the market by constantly being in touch with the head of the other departments.
10. Source information on the volatility estimates of the market to the seniors.
11. Keep updates of products of competitive companies.
12. Participate in various sales promotion programmers and organize such programmes in various States.

The marketing department, taking care of all the above points, means it will have to work on a war footing. In any business, the marketing department has to run around, the maximum. In this hectic running around too, the employees of this department have to always work with a pleasant look. Marketing department, in any business, is the face that confronts the market.

If a business is small, then the proprietor handles all the departments himself. But along with the development of the business, he has to develop various departments too. The development of the business will be as fast if the marketing department is modern and fresh.

To bring about such development, all kinds of marketing are put into use. Several businessmen easily introduce their products to the market. This is known as soft marketing. Customers will not know much or will not be shocked, when new products are introduced to the market in such a way. Several discounts are given, without much fanfare, to increase sales. One benefit of this is that customers will not even know when, after some time, these discounts are withdrawn. This soft marketing does not even alert the competitors. By the time they know of it, much time has already gone by.

The other method of marketing is aggressive marketing. In this kind of marketing, the attention of the customers is drawn instantly, and they will be shaken or it will be made a talking matter. The information of the product is reached to every home through putting up huge hoardings in the city or through house-to-house survey. Several attractive schemes are announced for the customers. Offers, of free gifts as per the cost of products purchased, one on one free or some grams free gold scheme, are announced. By studying markets in some cities, these schemes are announced in many cities, at the same time. In some important cities an exhibition of the manufactured products is held. The team of marketing officials takes great effort for this. They draw different schemes. In a way, marketing is a continuous process. The marketing department has an equal importance as the production department in any company. The marketing department endlessly impresses the quality of the product in the mind of people.

In the obsession with competition, businessmen indulge in negative marketing too. Instead of reaching the qualities of their own product to the customers, the marketing department spends its brain on talking about the faults of the competitors' products. Even if the momentary benefits of negative marketing may be visible, in the long run, this kind of marketing could be loss causing and hence dangerous. Companies, with intention of doing business for a long term and with a decided objective to build its influence in the market, should avoid such negative marketing.

> *"Be more concerned with your Character than your Reputation, because your Character is what you really are, while your Reputation is merely what others think you are."*
>
> **—John Wooden**

□

16

Advertising

"If people are not laughing at your goals, your goals are too small."

—**Azim Premji,** Founder of WIPRO

It is said that advertisement is the 65th art. No effective medium than advertisements can be found anywhere for imprinting a product in the mind of the people and to register it in their memory permanently. A good advertisement can find a permanent abode for your product in the mind of the people. The word Advertise is derived from the Latin word Ad vertere, which means 'to turn toward.' That means the main purpose of an advertisement is to draw attention of an individual or a community towards a product and to provoke the customer to purchase the product.

A business, big or small, has to advertise. Even though all the three, viz. marketing, public relation, and advertisement, are directly related to the manufactured product only, in practice, they are totally different. Their technique and formula are different. Marketing is theoretical and advertising is the visual effect of it. Many companies give equal importance to marketing and advertising, as to production. There are independent departments for both.

Advertisement is not merely a technique, it is also an art. Hence, even a simple, easy advertisement also can be ingrained in the people's mind for years and years. Basically, it is people's inborn, innate feeling to show a good thing with them to others or to draw attention of people to an important thing we have. Advertisement was born from this feeling. Initially, advertisements were crude and over a period of time began to be very attractive and beautiful. It has become objectively oriented. Businessmen realized the importance of advertisements for business and advertisements began to occupy a special place in the business. The importance of advertisements increased with the media revolution that took place in the last few years in the world. Electronic media reached advertisements to every home and being audio-visual it stayed on in the viewers' mind. People easily started humming jingles, heard on radio. A good advertisement came to be considered a value addition for the product.

An independent advertising department has been established in many businesses. At the same time, the assistance of some creative advertising agencies is sought. Competition grew in advertising. The struggle began to make advertising slogans more effective. Advertisements like, 'Giving homeliness to homes' of D.S.K. Builders, or 'let kalnirnay (decision about time) be on (your) wall' of the Kalniranay calendar or 'Building houses building Nation' of Haware Properties, reached every mind. These advertisements delivered perfectly.

Competition began in advertisements to rope in popular stars or artistes. The beats of Zakir Hussein on the tabla followed by his uttering 'wah Taj' won the appreciation of people for Tajmahal Tea. 'I have eaten the salt of the nation', this advertisement of Tata salt recalls memory, of the struggle for independence, for those who listen to it.

Businessman will have to be alert to change the advertisements with the times. Hence, these advertisements have to be changed constantly. Even though the advertisement of 'Nirma' has remained the same year after year, the girl artiste in it has been changed many times. Presently, even political parties have started following the advertising path. Political parties have started hammering advertisements very hard to influence voters' mind. Various parties have presented very clever advertising, being very proficient in wooing voters. Look how effectively the tagline 'Where have you taken My Maharashtra' has clicked in the recent elections in Maharashtra.

Whether the businessman is big or small, he has to advertise. Often a particular product is permanently ingrained in the consumers' mind. In his view, there is no alternative to the product. With the hammering of others' advertisements, this product could be forgotten. Hence, even these manufactures have to advertise.

Business owners have to constantly keep watch on preparing a good copy for advertising, getting a good jingle made, getting a good placement on prime time or in newspapers and such things. A long-term campaign is run to ingrain an advertisement into the mind of the people. Such campaigns penetrate everyone.

No business will have to confront failure if they mange the trio of quality product, clever marketing, and attractive advertising. In small businesses, it is a 'one man show.' There the owner only is the manager, the marketing chief and handles the advertising front. As the business grows, the necessity of establishing independent well-equipped departments will arise. A business can certainly run profitably if attention is paid to marketing and advertising departments while taking care of the quality of the product. Constant monitoring of the kind and quantum of response to advertisements, catchment area from where the response is coming, in that how much is the potential response and how much sales is impacted because of it has to be constantly done. By this it can be estimated as to advertising in which media, which time period and which geographical area evokes better response and this could help in doing a targeted advertising campaign. Thus, unnecessary advertising and costs on them can be avoided.

Today various media like television, radio, newspapers, periodicals, Internet, e-marketers hoarding, buses, mass e-mails, SMS and their variety are available in the market. Marketing on social media is a new trend. Here the advertising can be very targeted and it is cheaper too compared to other media. It is very important to select the right one among these.

Along with advertising, public relation (PR) has a very significant place in business. Publishing a news article about the same product in media creates a totally different image about the product. PR is Public Relations. It is dealing with all the people those are related with the product and business. It includes government officials and customers. Today PR agencies are available to cater to these needs. The best brand building of a business can be done with a perfect blend of advertising and public relations.

> *"The common question that gets asked in business is, 'why?' That's a good question, but an equally valid question is, 'why not?'"*
>
> —**Jeff Bezos,** CEO of Amazon

□

17

The Leader

"The best leader is the one who has sense enough to pick good men to do what he wants done, and the self restraint to keep from meddling with them, while they do it."

—**Theodore Roosevelt,** 26th President of USA

There is a very good Sanskrit shloka:
Amantram Aksharam Nasti,
Nasti Mool Manaushadham |
Ayogya Purusho Nasti,
Yojakastatra Durlabhaha | |

Meaning that, there is not a single word that does not have the power of the mantra. There is not a single plant that does not have an herbal quality and not a single man or woman who is useless. The only thing lacking is a leader the organiser. Leaders are rare.

Any business is started to make it successful. And all the responsibility of that success lies on the leadership of that business. The leader is like a warrior, ever ready to combat with weapons in both hands. Just as he is crowned with the glory of victory, so also he has to accept the infamy of defeat. In a way, he is the all in all of the business. Therefore, he has to be a complete leader.

Veteran researcher businessman and experienced military personnel Jagadish Kumar, in his book *How to Create a Winning Organization* has compared business with war. He states that the study of management science was first started in the military. Soldiers have to be prepared round the clock for the security of the nation. Several times the army is called to handle difficult situations even within nation. During peacetime, the research for new weapons and ammunitions and practice goes on continuously. The chief has to always take care that the soldiers' loyalty and mental strength are sustained forever. In modern time the military chief has to be in preparedness always, keeping in mind the future of tomorrow. Thus, he should have foresight. He has to constantly fight to manipulate to defeat/counter rivals and for this he has to constantly keep his soldiers on alert. Allocating tasks to every group a watch has to be kept on them at various levels. Taking note of the rival's preparations, necessary changes in our defense arsenal should be made. Various schemes have to be worked out to improve the quality of every group from the military officers to soldiers. Finding out the weak links in his force, he should adopt effective measures to strengthen them.

In any business, the leadership there has to do exactly this. The war-like situation or period of war is short in the military. But in business it is always a war-like situation. The situation has become more challenging due to globalization. The competition in the modern market, that affirms 'Customer alone is our God,' has become very stiff. Hence, businessmen have to be very alert constantly about the quality, trust, and availability of any of their products. They have to always take care to see how their product is better than that of their competitors. Thus, businessmen have to always be in war-like situation. Hence, several aspects of war management and leadership become applicable to business in the very same manner.

Some things become indispensable for the growth of business. The company owner and chief officers should decide the objectives of the company and communicate it properly to the employees. They should allocate responsibility of each one's work and minutely watch time and again whether they are being executed properly, to attain the company's objectives. A time-bound programme should be scheduled to fulfill the objectives and should be executed through a managing system. A close watch has to be kept on the competitors and their every move should be observed. The employees should always be kept prepared, constantly looking out for business opportunities. They should give thought to constantly improving quality to meet new challenges. Necessary training should be given regularly to improve managing quality. Effecting necessary change in the company's technology and plant and machinery, they should always be kept modernized. For this the company's Research and Development team has to always be forthcoming. Efforts should be made to see that every employee's loyalty and love for the company remain constant in their mind. So also every employee should be properly instructed about this work and the same should be got done in the specified time. A systematic effort should be made to find and capture markets for the manufactured products. Any business is a continuous process and the responsibility of its success lies with its leadership.

Businessman should have all necessary qualities of leadership. Leadership has to take care of taking decisions, building a team with right people, encouraging them after understanding their quality, confronting new changes and not ever allowing to swerve from the viewpoint of development. For this a CEO can be appointed. Though many people, who decorate this post, have those qualities inbred, yet many try to sincerely attain them.

The company's scope of work has widened due to globalization. Hence, the work of a CEO too has undergone several changes. Earlier a CEO gave 70 percent of his time for the company and 30 percent of his time for outside work. Today the CEO has to do reverse. For most of his time he has to spend in communicating with investors, the government, politicians, foreign guests, and social workers. Hence, delegating his work to others, he has to find time for other work. He has to draw schemes to give opportunity to his associates after recognizing their merit. For this a CEO has to have a good recognition of people, and also the goodness of mind to take them all with him together. He has to show his skill to look after the interests of his company while negotiating with representatives of other big companies. Increasing exports is essential for the development of export-oriented companies. For this he has to study markets in various countries. He has to be very careful while entering into agreement with foreign companies. From this point of view only, businessmen should have complete knowledge and information.

On the basis of such information, only he can cleverly negotiate and serve the company's interests. At the same time, he has to keep communicating with the investors, customers, distributors, and other such levels. A CEO's objective should be to have good communication among employees, increase their efficiency and thereby reach good products to the customers. Having accepted leadership, the CEO cannot give any excuses. He has to be always prepared, to work for hours and hours, not to be able to give much time to his family and to go outstation or abroad. As Dr. Raghunath Mashelkar puts it, like any leader a CEO has to mainly have three qualities – compassion in the heart, creativity in the mind, and the yearning for progress within. Due to this alone, his success can get a humanitarian hue.

In a way, a CEO has to be a complete leader. The CEO has to be effective from all points of view – thought, foresight, reputation, and image. The imagination power of any CEO has to be able to attain distinctive heights than his associates. He should be able to amaze his associates with his high thinking. However, this thinking should not be inscrutable or daydreaming. This thought should have objectives that are possible with due efforts. Even then it should have the dimensions of distinctiveness, innovation, and curiosity. Though it is difficult, his associates should have the confidence that he can achieve it.

He should have a scheme to implement his ideas. He will have to be able to make an action plan. More importantly, those implementing the plan should feel that it is within their capacity. He should have the clever intelligence to make everybody accept the plan. Also it should not be merely imaginative, but should have his experience added to it. It is a common experience that without experience, mere words prove futile. It is very difficult to convince associates about his scheme and encouraging them to actually do the work. But those who want be leader, should be able to make this possible easily. This means they should be able to thrust their ideas into their associates easily. To implement their ideas, they have to select a worthy team. For this, they should be able to evaluate people. They have to inspire the team for their objective and have the tact to make them feel that this objective is the only goal of their life.

To be able to have influence over their associates, they should have total information of the work and the capacity to solve issues and help wherever they are stuck. For this they should maintain as much contact as possible with the employees of the company. They should inadvertently note the merits-demerits of every employee and the status of work in every department. This information serves their purpose of governance. The able and efficient employees should be given more scope by giving them newer responsibilities. While doing so only, they should give more scope to varied ideas. From this alone innovative ideas will emerge.

Even though the CEO has all authority, he should never close the doors of his mind. Instead he should himself develop the habit of listening to others. Through such listening alone, a very new idea sometimes is put forth. Also the person has the satisfaction of the highest official having listened to him. With this one act, half their grievances are eliminated. A feeling of confidence and belonging is built. A true leader is one who listens to others and such leaders alone are successful in their career. Whether the business is big or small – the individual who heads the business should nourish the above things within him.

'Leadership should not be thrust, it should be accepted. For this the leader has to enhance his capacity to listen.'

"If you really want to do something, you will find a way. If you don't, you will find an excuse."

– **Jim Rohn,** American entrepreneur, author and motivational speaker

□

18

Before Stepping Back

"Education is the milk of a tigress. Those who drink it, will certainly roar."

—Bharat Ratna Dr. Babasaheb Ambedkar

The youth completing his education and entering the struggle of life is a bit flummoxed. Traditional convention has told him to go ahead in a rut (particular routine) and to get familiar with that rut, but the exuberant young mind is not ready to mutely listen to it. The clamor of emotions and new ideas are built in his mind. The passion in his mind is craving to do something different. He is not prepared to accept a stuck in the rut or insipid life. The decision that he takes at the deciding moment of his life will be the turning point of his life. There itself he will find a new direction. The yearning to practically realize the dreams of the mind is created.

Exactly at the very same time the seed, to do something and show, germinates in the mind of the youth. The change in thoughts has occurred like the economic change due to globalization. The number of people, wanting to do something distinct from others instead of the traditional things, is growing day by day. The yearning for creating something new is making the mind of such youth restless. From this begins the mental and intellectual churn. Much brainstorming commences. The need to get proper direction is at this very time.

Many times the mind is in a drifting like state at such times. Several different paths beckon. Varied attractions keep enticing. Direction is not found at this specific time. If one decides to do something, there is nothing in the hand to do it. No guide is available. Friends and relatives utter list of hurdles. It becomes impossible to take decisions.

If a person caught in such a whirlwind of thoughts, finds the proper path, then his whole life transforms. The objective of this book is to help him find this path. The youth in such a restless state many times think of being drawn to the path of business. Of them, many also come to the decision of doing independent business or profession. But at the very opportune moment their confidence collapses. They start seeing darkness in front of their eyes. They are unable to decide whether to take the plunge or not. They do not have much capital with them. They are unsure of the future. Many people retract at this stage itself. They seal their future prospects with their own hands. This book is only for those who are in the mental state of stepping back. It is written so that they do not step back.

The objective of this book is to give a friendly advice 'start from where you are and first utilize what you have at hand'. The objective of this writing is to give a positive direction to those who are confused, about what first step to take in which direction and when, while starting the journey of life. The highest creation of wealth of the nation is from the business sector. Hence, it is always said that instead of pursuing jobs, youth should turn to business. But when the youth stands at the threshold of the prime of his life, then several questions confront him. He gets confused with the very thought of the challenges there. He does not have much backing of money. His slate of experience is empty. At such a time it is essential to tell him four things intimately. It becomes essential to give mind a lift. Caught in the anxiety of how he could plunge into the vast ocean with not much money in his pocket, when somebody tells him "business should be done on others' money only, it should not be done with one's own money; there are many ways to get money", then he will momentarily be shocked with surprise, but he will also start thinking in that direction. Such is somewhat the state of the first-generation businessmen too.

He is aware of the obstacles in a job, but he becomes restless by small-big hurdles while doing business. In this state, do not fear the raids conducted by the government departments or the phone call from goons. These youth should be taken into confidence by someone and told that keeping their transactions clean they can firmly confront these hurdles. Someone should also provide them information on planning, management, marketing, and advertisement. This written discourse is for this.

Most important of all is that business is the issue of the pride of a nation. Any businessman should feel in his mind that by running a business successfully, they are doing a great service to the nation. Business should be done with a sense of pride and self-respect. It is directly related to national service and social service. Businessmen can face any challenges if they do business by abiding by all laws and without blemish, this confidence should be aroused in the mind of such bewildered youth.

They should study in depth about the process of erecting a business, putting together plant and machinery, time-bound planning, recruitment of employees and actual production and its distribution. But once they are slightly acquainted with all these, the steps of those intending to enter this sector will fall with more self-confidence. Ultimately, it is their own decision as to what path to take. Capable persons select their path themselves and putting all their might into it and become successful.

Field Marshal Sam Manekshaw, in fact, wanted to go abroad and study, but his father opposed him, as he felt that how could he send such a small lad abroad alone. Therefore, he joined the army in anger for proving his ability, rose to become a field marshal. He proved his capability. Success becomes much easy, when you do a thing that convinces your mind.

Veteran businessmen G.D. Birla and Walchand Hirachand selected their path at a very young age, as per their own liking. Birla stepped out of his family business at the age of 15 only. He became an agent for selling jute. Walchand became a construction contractor at the age of 20. Walchand accepted his first work of constructing a seven km railway line track. He accepted this work against the wishes of his father. He worked very hard in the initial stages to prove himself. Riding on the donkey, he was supervising the construction work, that, he got initially of the seven km railway line. He called this donkey, the Butkya. He maintained this donkey till the end of his life.

He was always in touch with Gandhi, Nehru, and Patel. Hence, even while expanding his business empire, he presented an example of patriotism. Those starting a profession should be reminded that the ultimate objective of any profession should be service to the nation and service to the society only. "A trader's first God is his business and working hard and serving for that is his duty", these words of Walchand should be carved in the mind of all aspiring to come into this field for the first time. Walchand only started the Scindia Steam Navigation Company. The day he commissioned his first ship 'The Loyalty', that day is observed today as India's 'National Maritime Day'. This man, who started with a seven km railway line, goes to open factories to build ships and aeroplanes. He meets the likes of Goering and Henry Ford, the youth should understand this. The commissioning of the ship 'The Loyalty' was done at the hands of Jawaharlal Nehru. Aspiring businessmen should know that Walchand always saw to it that his business was related to nationalism.

The memory of J.R.D. Tata, whose attitude was 'it is better to lose a project than to give bribe or to stoop', should be reminded about to the youth. 'While executing any work, try to scale the highest heights and never compromise on the quality'. The Tata business group could establish an empire of thousands of crores by following this principle alone. This story should always be before us like a slogan.

Is it not inspiring to the youth that Dhirubhai Ambani, who established the Reliance business group empire of several crores, worked initially in a petrol pump? Even after such a great successful journey, Dhirubhai's attitude was of humility. Dhirubhai used to say, "I consider myself to be a searcher of path. Surveying the jungle, I prepare a path so that people can tread in future." "I will keep working till my last breath. For retirement there is only one place, that is the crematorium", who will not be inspired by these words of Dhirubhai? These businessmen, who have scaled heights of success in the business field, had an equally high level of integrity and fairness.

The example of businessman Kasturbhai Lalchand is as inspiring. When one of his relatives did embezzlement, he lodged a police complaint and gave witness too against him. In 1953, Union Commerce and Industry Ministry sent him a cheque of 88 rupees and 12 annas for his railway journey from Mumbai to Ahmedabad. This amount was in excess of one rupee. Hence, his secretary sent a one-rupee note back to the Union Ministry.

The ideal of Tata and Kasturbhai will certainly keep the youth coming to the field of business on the path of integrity. The popularity of Bajaj scooters at one point of time was at its peak. During that time people had to book Bajaj scooters 8-10 years in advance. Bajaj scooters had become a status symbol then. At that time people would have accepted whatever increase in price of the scooter. But Rahul Bajaj, the president of Bajaj Scooters refused to increase the price. He stated, "our objective is to provide vehicles at lesser cost and we will never leave this motto". Raids were conducted on this very Bajaj out of political vengeance. His 144 offices were raided at the same time in 1976. They also conducted enquiry of his 84-year-old grandmother Janakidevi. Aspiring officials entering the profession should be aware of the integrity of businessmen and the hardships they undergo. But also efforts should be made to completely do away with raids.

Even Ram Prasad Goenka, Baba Kalyani, the sons of great businessmen had to start their employment on a monthly salary of 250-300 rupees. This information will certainly ground those who entertain unrealistic ideas about financial income. Dr. Raghunath Mashelkar, the director general of C.S.I.R. and senior scientist once said, "We can no longer afford to remain poor. Creating wealth is our responsibility and for that the real need is to convert our knowledge into wealth." And businessmen do just that.

If every individual firmly thrust this principle into his mind then poverty will vanish from our country in no time. There is no other alternative to wealth creation than business. If this sentiment is aroused in every youth coming out after completing his education, then the issues of poverty and unemployment will be solved in no time.

Keeping this objective in mind, several businessmen of the country did their business successfully and in a way dedicated it to the nation. From G.D. Birla, Jamshedji Tata, J.R.D. Tata, Walchand Hirachand, Rama Durai, R.P. Goenka, Rahulkumar Bajaj, Aabasaheb Garware, Shantanurao Kirloskar to the very present generation's Bedekar, Dandekar, Chitale, Pendharkar, many businessmen with extra-ordinary talent and endless hard work built up their business empires. A big share of credit for the building of India, post-independence, must go to these businessmen. Of course, all those who enter this profession cannot be like them. They have to bear the heat and hard knock of their situation. Many a time they are flung into the abyss of failure. Many a time they are carried away by their success. Many a time the steps taken with purity and confidence have to be retracted. By giving practical examples of people around, at such a time, and if a true light of their world is shown, then certainly there could be a positive impact. He not only realizes the sheer strength of this world but also the pitfalls here. The understanding is created in his mind that by properly planning if the business is well organized then success is not far off. This written discourse is to motivate the mind to organize it so. In some pictures, some lines are depicted with dots. An aspiring artist has to join the dots with a pencil. This book is to prepare one's mind to join the dots of the line. It is said that anything first enters the mind and then practically accomplished. It is important that the mind should be prepared. That means we do everything twice, first we do it in mind and then in reality. So doing business without money is not difficult. There is only a need that you first decide to do that in mind. And be sure that it will be a reality next.

"The world suffers a lot. Not because of the violence of the bad people,
But because of the silence of good people!"

—Napoleon

□

Have a Great Idea. But No Money? Do not let that Stop You!

There are several beliefs and misconceptions and a kind of curiosity about business in our society. The author has elucidated many such business-related beliefs in this book in a very amusing way, as also cited incidents encouraging the youth to start their own ventures. Dr. Suresh Haware has breached the general understanding among people that business can only be done if backed by money power. Capital can be raised from outside, rather, it should be raised from outside sources only. The main Capital that one should compulsorily have to do business is that of the rare willpower, of self-confidence and business attitude! In order to imbibe this basic mantra, he discusses the required elements, in detail, in this book to raise hopes to do business.

The important subjects that he has delved upon in this book include – how to establish a business, how to design and implement it, branding, relations, budget of the business and how to plan and grow. Those who learn from their own experience are considered clever, but those who learn from others' experience are the truly intelligent people. Hence, these words of experience will certainly be very useful for the youth wanting to set up a new business or those wanting to progress in business. Businessmen are the main segment that create national wealth, opines Dr. Haware with full self-confidence. The words of experience of Dr. Haware, who has successfully managed all affairs of the construction business for many years, will certainly be inspiring and guiding to aspiring businessmen.

□□□